Sweet Sound

The Power of Discipling
Kids in Worship

Powerful, Practical, and Prophetic

Yancy Wideman Richmond

Sweet Sound - The Power of Discipling Kids in Worship

Published by Yancy Ministries, Inc. 2441-Q Old Fort Pkwy #354 Murfreesboro, TN 37128 USA. Yancy and Yancynotnancy are registered trademarks.

This title may be purchased in bulk for educational, business, fundraising or sales promotional use. For information, please email info@yancyministries.com.

ISBN 978-1-7378454-0-9
ISBN (eBook) 978-1-7378454-1-6
ISBN (Audio) 978-1-7378454-2-3

Library of Congress Control Number: TXu002279118

Cover Design by Hampton Creative
Book Layout by Nicole Jones
Author Photo by Hannah Corwin
Make-up by Whitney LeGrand

YancyMinistries.com

Printed in the United States of America

Table of
Contents

By Kari Jobe

"The other day, I think God held my hands in worship!"

I looked at Canyon, my oldest son, his eyes full of wonder.

"Where were you?" I asked him.

He told me he was at kid's church. He showed me how he closed his eyes and put his hands high into the air. Then he said, "I felt someone holding my hands."

"Wow, Canyon, that's amazing!" My mother's heart was so excited for him. "Yes, I loved it." He replied, "Do you think that was God or the Holy Spirit?"

What a beautiful question. I told him, "Baby, God is everywhere but the Holy Spirit is the One He sent to comfort us and be our best friend. I think it was Holy Spirit." And Canyon went, "Yea, I think so too."

I love everything about that story and what my precious son experienced. I believe the beauty and power of worship is something that's already coming alive in him, a hunger for the presence of God and a desire to know Him more.

I remember when I was a young girl, not much older than Canyon, and how I loved everything about worship because I started realizing its ability to reveal God and His presence in such special ways.

One night, my parents were ministering to a couple going through a hardship in their marriage. They had me sit in the car while they were talking and praying with them. As I did, a song came on the radio and every word related to the situation. It was like the Holy Spirit had the right song come on at the right time, and it felt so tangible in the car.

At that moment, I realized how powerful songs can be, how they can help people pray and experience breakthrough. I remember telling God, "I want to do this. I want to write songs that help people encounter You."

Now, it's taken years to develop the calling God placed on my life. Soon after that night, the children's worship leader at my church asked if I would lead worship in kid's church. He asked me to work on a set list, so I thought long and hard about what I wanted to do and what songs would be familiar and easy for kids to sing along to.

Ready to see what I chose?

1. *B-I-N-G-O*
2. *John Jacob Jingle Heimer Schmidt*
3. *Jesus Loves Me*

When I shared that set list with my parents, they got a good laugh! I had a lot to learn, and they graciously helped me. Eventually, we changed the set list to two simple, yet intentional, songs: *I Love You Lord* and *Jesus Loves Me*.

I share this because I've realized firsthand how important it is to cultivate an atmosphere for the presence of God to move, especially for children at a young age.

I experienced it in my parent's car because my mom and dad would play worship music almost everywhere we were. Worship wasn't something we did once a week at church. Worship was our lifestyle and God was given room to move in me as a result.

Canyon experienced this at our church because our pastors and leaders cultivate an atmosphere for God's presence. They repeatedly tell the kids and adults, "There's no junior Holy Spirit," so the kids believe that. They know that even though they're young, that doesn't mean they can't encounter God.

Undoubtedly, there's a reason Jesus said, "Let the little children come to me." (Matthew 19:14) Childlike faith unreservedly loves. It delightfully trusts. It unashamedly longs to leap into the arms of Jesus and soak up every moment in His presence.

That's why I'm so grateful and excited this book is in your hands. It's my heart's cry to always create space for the sacred, to make room for God to move in and through His people in supernatural ways. And I know it's Yancy's as well.

We both go to the same church, The Belonging Co in Nashville, TN. We both have young kids who we pray will always walk in relationship with their heavenly Father. And we both see the need to cultivate worship in their young hearts.

We know there's no junior Holy Spirit because we've experienced firsthand His ability to speak and work through His kids. And in this book you're going to read not just Yancy's personal story and what God has revealed to her about worship, but also His heart to move through you and the practical ways you can cultivate the sweet sound of children's worship, helping them encounter His presence in life-changing ways.

In Matthew 5, verses 6 and 8, Jesus says, *"Blessed are those who hunger and thirst after righteousness for they will be filled... Blessed are the pure in heart for they will see God."*

It's my deepest desire for my kids to hunger and thirst after God. To walk in purity that they may see Him in all His beauty and holiness. That's why I want to set a worshipful atmosphere around them, that they might know the presence of God and recognize Him as the Source for everything they need in life.

Think of it as a meal. If I'm not intentional about the food I set before them each day, they're going to gravitate to the sweet stuff, to candy and desserts, which while fun to eat, aren't going to give them the nutrients they need to grow. So, I help them. I set the table. I prepare a meal that's going to help them develop as healthy boys.

Similarly, that's what this book will equip you to do for the children you have the honor and privilege to lead. You'll learn how to "set a table" that won't just be fun for them to experience but intentional in its elements to help them encounter what they need, which is God's presence in worship.

He always comes where He's invited. He works where He's given space to move. He releases His presence when we worship. And whether you're a pastor, leader, parent, or student, I'm praying the Holy Spirit will speak to you clearly in the pages ahead that Yancy has so prayerfully and anointedly written.

As you experience God's tangible, wonderful, life-changing presence, may you cultivate an atmosphere for kids to fill the air with a sweet sound of worship.

—Kari Jobe

The Sweetest
Sound

I'll never forget the power of a dad's words. He came early to pick his daughter up from our kids worship team rehearsal. He stood in the back watching and waiting, while we finished practicing for the service that weekend. As he watched, our kids worship team was singing their hearts out. This dad looked me in the face afterward and said, "There is power in their worship. Adults could learn a lot from watching children worship." That day, he left differently than when he had first walked in. He had seen something that felt unfamiliar to his adult mind. The children worshiping had impacted him, and he was changed.

I don't know if you've had the fortunate experience to be in a room with a group of kids while they participate in worship, but it is the sweetest sound you will ever hear. Their voices united. Singing with love. Completely pure. Giving who they are for the glory of God.

It's in this moment that they are doing the very thing they were knit together in their mother's womb to do. Praising their Maker who knows everything about them. He counts every hair, numbers every day, and bottles every tear in a bottle.

When they sing, demons flee.

When they worship, darkness is drowned out by the light.

When they posture their heart for the delight of the Father, they are resting in His arms. The arms of their Savior. They are known. They are loved. And they are responding to His love with their awe and wonder. It's in these moments where they are living out the famous psalm that David wrote: "May the words of my mouth and the meditation of my heart be pleasing to you, O Lord, my rock and my redeemer." (Psalm 19:14, NLT)

Our worship is for His delight.

Our testimony is for His glory.

The posture of our heart toward Him is where we are transformed. When we draw close, He draws close. Worshiping God is the most natural thing we can do. Just like our bodies were made to breathe, our spirits were made to praise the King of kings and Lord of lords. When we don't respond in worship, I believe His heart is grieved. As a parent delights in the love of their child, we have a Father in heaven who desires nothing more than to engage in an exchange of affection with His children.

I can picture our preteen classroom. I was standing in the back of the room, watching the team lead our students. Something happened to me. Our kids were singing out in worship with all their hearts. It was a song that paraphrased the stanza repeated in Psalms 136: "He is good and His love endures forever." In all of my young adult naivety and headstrong determination, I was moved. I was changed. I knew the sound I was hearing was special. It was Creation roaring the praises of their Creator. It was lives that had been saved by grace, declaring they are redeemed. Our 5th & 6th graders were engaged in lifting their voices in worship. They weren't too cool to use their voices to sing what they knew was true. I heard the sweetest sound. My eyes filled with tears, just as they have hundreds of times since at the sweet sound of children singing in worship.

In the season I knew I was to write this book, but had not yet begun the writing process, I got a text from a friend one day, letting me know that she was praying for my words. That text was exactly what my heart needed because, little did she know, I had been secretly making excuses for why I couldn't write it. I'm a songwriter. I'm only a singer. Isn't it silly how we fight ourselves with our own thoughts and lies? I already knew the title of this book would be "Sweet Sound." Then, that same morning, in the middle of the conference I was attending, they went into the chorus of the worship song, "I Love You Lord."

"Let it be a sweet, sweet sound in Your ear."

I knew I couldn't run any longer. These ideas and thoughts have taken my whole life, thus far, to learn. They are a reflection of my heart, but even more so, they are a glimpse of His heart.

I pray you are changed as you read these words. I pray that you gain fresh vision for what God has in store for the kids you are entrusted to lead. But more than anything, I pray that the sound of your life and the worship you express each day is a sweet sound!

The song you were made to sing has been sung in the heavenlies since the beginning of time, and it will be sung forever into eternity. The song of worship is already playing, and now this is your invitation to sing.

Holy holy holy
Lord God, Almighty
Early in the morning,
Our song shall rise to Thee.

This is what you were made for.
And the beat goes on.

I Love Jesus:
My Story

Chapter One

I love Jesus. I felt the need to put that out there in the open, first & foremost. At this point in my life, I can say with all sincerity that He alone is my goal and my reason. Years ago, I began describing my music as music that makes Jesus loud. I'm all about a song that can rock out a bit. I believe God's Word is true when it tells us to shout to God with a voice of triumph (Psalm 47:1). But whether the song is loud or quiet, my desire remains unchanged. I have one goal and one goal alone: To declare the praises of my King with my entire being.

I truly believe there is no sweeter sound in the entire world than to hear a group of children singing out in praise to the Father. It's pure and innocent, and it's true. It's the sound that each of us were created to sing. Worship is ingrained in our DNA. Worship to the Father is what we were wired to do and to give back to Him.

I'm a church girl, through & through. It's where I spent my days beginning at an early age in Jackson, Mississippi. On a hot and muggy July day, they hung a giant pink bow on a weeping willow tree outside of the church where my father worked. Yes, it was clearly a handful of decades ago, long before a photo could be posted on social media or a text could be sent on a smartphone. I feel like that giant pink bow for all to see reveals a lot about my personality. God is in the details, y'all. I was born in the Church. It's the place where I navigated and accomplished every phase of my life. I am passionate about championing the Church to be what God has created us to be, and the Bride He is coming back for.

I've been a lover of music from my early years. There's photographic evidence of me as a preschooler with my Mr. Microphone toy performing on the stage (aka: the fireplace hearth) in the living room of our home in Birmingham, Alabama. Our Church had a recording studio during the time that would have been more of a rarity. Today, we have the ability to make music on a laptop. Nashville alone, where I currently live, has a long list of home studios. What I'm referring to was a real twenty-four track studio recording on tape. Even as I write this, the dots are connecting that this is the place where the desires within me were first ignited.

My dad, Jim Wideman, was a children's pastor beginning in the late 1970s. My sister and I would spend time with him on Saturdays as he prepared for Sunday morning and the kids he would minister to. I can still picture the chapel where we had kid's church in Montgomery, Alabama. It was the place where I sang on the worship team for the first time. There was team practice every Saturday afternoon. One week, someone was unable to make it to practice, so I volunteered to fill their spot. That led to buying accompaniment tracks at our local Christian bookstore, and then practicing a special song, over & over, to sing to my peers. I still remember the details of that first performance. I sang "You're the Same," by an artist known at the time as Leslie Phillips. The lyrics, "You're the same forever, yesterday and today, You will love me this way, cause your heart never changes," impacted me in a profound way.

Fast forward to the Sunday evening service where I sang my first solo with the children's choir. It was a legend of a song that most churchgoers will know well: "Awesome God," by Rich Mullins.

Sweet Sound

"When He rolled up His sleeves, He ain't just puttin' on the ritz." No one writes lyrics like that anymore. I was forever marked. It was around this same time that I began to realize that music was what I was made to do. I like to say it like this: As confident as I am that my name is Yancy, I know that God created me to sing and create music. For the next 15 years of my story, I was a part of every worship team and band at church that I could possibly join. Whether it was singing in children's choirs, sharing the offertory, or performing a special song that I had performed hundreds of times before, while rehearsing in my bedroom in front of the mirror, of course. God bless my family for enduring the sounds that came from my room. I literally mimicked every Amy Grant song that came out. Along with singing, I also incorporated playing piano. Just before I turned ten, we moved to Tulsa, Oklahoma. I started taking piano lessons from a new teacher. I am a firm believer that the right teacher makes all the difference. This man changed everything for me. It's hard to fully comprehend what he saw, but I'm convinced that Willie Davis knew at least a taste of my destiny. I don't know if Holy Spirit had given him a vision or if he just knew I was marked, but there's no doubt that he saw something in me and called it out. I'm pretty sure he had me playing in the kids worship band only a few months later. He set the bars for me, and I would rise up to each one. I don't say this to boast, but instead, to stand in awe and highlight the significance that leaders play in the lives of children. He kept training me, and the opportunities to play and sing kept coming. I would serve on worship teams leading my peers and, at times, those older than me, which included playing keyboard for our college group.

Somewhere along the way, I began leading worship for middle schoolers, which to this day, I stand by my opinion that they are the hardest age group to lead. It's the only area where I begged my parents to let me quit. Middle schoolers at 9am on a Sunday are just tough. They were next to impossible to lead. But, of course, my parents didn't let me give up. That experience toughened me and better prepared me to lead worship for a group of people that lack the desire to be there. There are certainly times where you need the ability to get on stage and perform your best, even if your audience is not responsive, and possibly even looks annoyed to be there. Thanks to those middle schoolers, I developed that skill set.

Looking back on it now, it feels a bit like a snowball that continued to grow bigger and bigger. Opportunities were given to me to develop my abilities. When I reflect back, it feels like every adult in my life knew what I was born for. The ministry volunteers in every area of our church cheered me on. They championed me in my calling. Their words and belief were fanning the flame inside me to do this thing called "music."

I eventually recorded my first album, "Big Weather Change," the summer before my senior year of high school. I started traveling the country performing for youth groups. I'd show up to their youth service and put on a concert. That was the beginning of my public ministry.

I started developing relationships in Nashville, TN. I made multiple trips back and forth from Oklahoma, writing songs and recording demos of songs, and knocking on doors of publishers and record labels. All was going well in my little dream bubble of music. I even received a couple cuts by some "real" artists (aka: Jaci Velasquez and Avalon). The latter recorded a song I wrote, "I Don't Want to Go," that went #1 on the charts for five weeks.

Everything was pretty much going as planned. About a year before I got married, I was given an opportunity to start leading worship as my full-time job. I needed to be home to lead on Wednesday nights, and then I'd do my CCM music stuff the rest of the time. However, over the next couple of years, one day led to a couple of days, which then led to a very consuming full-time job at our church. I was convinced that's where I was supposed to be, so I embraced it. As far as I was concerned, it's where I would be the rest of my life. I would die in my old age after living a full life leading worship for this church. I was leading teams of musicians and vocalists, as well as mentoring worship leaders to lead for every age group, all while physically helping to lead our main adult services on Sunday mornings. I was having a blast because I was engrossed in music almost every day of the week. But, I'm not gonna lie. I would occasionally be confused as to why I had gone back and forth to Nashville if I was only going to land back at full-time church work. What was the purpose in learning how to write real songs and record them if I wasn't going to be using any of that? There were days where I honestly wondered if I had missed it. Where did I make a mistake previously?

We performed at a very high bar. Our church was known for excellence. I don't say that to a fault, because I don't believe it is. Yes, it meant that I was responsible for a lot. Yes, it meant that I was surrounded by incredibly talented people who operated in this sort of ocean of creativity. Accomplishing "awesome" was a persona. This environment gave me plenty of opportunities through the years, and I was now getting to be a key part. I was working for someone incredibly talented who had come from a successful CCM career. What I learned as a vocalist, worship leader, and worship pastor was invaluable.

I loved my team something fierce. Like a "Mama Bear fights for her cubs" fierce. These students and young adults were the first children I ever mothered and led. And, I did it with my whole heart. I no doubt made some mistakes along the way. It seems impossible in my mid-twenties to have led them perfectly. But, even now, when I tell you that I loved those musicians, singers, and worship leaders, know that tears are filling my eyes.

As I said before, there were days where I would experience tension. It was hard. It stretched me. It grew me unlike anything else. Like many churches, we were in a season of change. I was part of the team that had been hired for where we were heading, but our feet were still stuck in some muddy waters of what had been. Some days it didn't feel like it was moving fast enough. In those moments, I couldn't see exactly what God was doing. But, even on the hard, tension-filled days, I had peace that I was exactly where I was supposed to be, so I kept my hand to the plow.

I know now that it's possible to have peace in the midst of tension. Those two things can and do coexist at times. The tension I experienced did not negate the peace that I also felt. I think as Christ followers, we believe that being in God's will means that we will never wrestle. On the side of this particular part of my story, I know confidently that God was still equipping me with skills that I needed for the future He had for me. Yes, I had *served* on worship teams for practically my entire life, but I was now *leading* teams. I was mentoring worship leaders. Some would start with our kids and end up leading in our adult services. Others would help me with high schoolers one night and preteens on the weekend. It was a season that I honestly wouldn't trade for anything. I spent my entire life around children's ministry. I had been to more conferences about the subject than I could count. I can confidently say that neither I, nor my parents, ever thought, *"Hey, Yancy should take this music thing and mix it with the kids ministry thing. That would be brilliant."* It never crossed my mind! I promise you. But God…

A few years prior, I began writing the theme song for a kid's summer camp program. There were 10,000 children who attended this camp every summer, and each year we had a theme with an original song. After camp was over, the song sort of lived on the shelf (outside of the people that had attended camp). After a few years, I realized I could obtain permission to use those masters, plus add a few new songs to the mix, and make a children's album. I still had no concrete vision for myself in that space. I just knew these were songs that held potential for other churches to use. Remember, I'm a PK and our church held many conferences where other churches came to gain knowledge & training. I knew kid's pastors and could easily get this music into their hands. That was as far as my vision went.

In 2006, I created my "Loud & Clear" album. It was full of the summer camp songs, plus a couple others that I had performed for my friend, Reggie Joiner, who started the organization, Orange, in Atlanta. I also recorded a cover of a Lincoln Brewster praise song, which was newly popular at the time, and wrote a few more songs for this "kid's album." A couple months after I released it, I went to the camp on a Monday to sing, and my voice was completely broken. When I say broken, I mean it sounded like my hand was randomly hitting keys on a piano and couldn't control the pitch that was coming out. I was puzzled. Everything was normal the day before. I remember the sound guy asking me what was wrong during sound check and having absolutely no clue. I went outside and called my dad to grill him with questions. Back in his college days, my dad had nodules on his vocal cords that resulted in surgery. In this scary moment, I wondered if what I was experiencing was some version of that. I remember asking him, "What happened when…?" I stayed and attempted to sing, but it was possibly one of the worst public performances of my life. The next day, I went to the doctor and she diagnosed it as allergies, plus gave me something to dry them out. (Probably the worst possible thing we could have done.) I realized that it was only the top four notes of my register that were affected, so I did what any full-time church employee who loved to sing would do: I lowered the keys of every song and continued to sing, making sure not to use any of those sketchy notes. I kept that going for about a month and things didn't get any better. So, I decided to call up a vocal coach in Nashville who I had previously seen. She wisely sent me to an ENT doctor who used a scope and saw that my vocal cords were swollen. This freaked me out since I knew that was the same diagnosis of Audio Adrenaline's lead singer who could no longer sing. I was given the prescription of "no singing" for a month, plus as many hours as I could of total vocal rest each week. So, every Thursday evening until Saturday afternoon, I would not speak. I highly recommend a Magna Doodle if you ever find yourself on some form of vocal rest. They are a very handy and practical solution for communication. Much to my dismay, my husband likes to act like he can't read my lips. I love him anyway! Magically, my parents and sister could always read my lips!

I had no idea what my future looked like. I wasn't fully confident that I had a future. Maybe I was going to be one of those stories you hear about the "former singer who no longer had the skills." I remember going to church and lip syncing during the worship. I didn't want to simply stand there. I was made to worship, and I was going to engage in worship even if there was no sound allowed to come out of my mouth. During this season, our church was singing a Chris Tomlin arrangement of the hymn, "I Stand Amazed." Passion had released it on their "Hymns" record sometime that year. I remember weeping at the lyric, "And my song shall ever be," because I truly had no idea if I'd ever be a vocalist again. Every time there was a lyric that involved singing, I would pray, "Jesus, I want to sing for you." When you're in desperate situations, you start praying some desperate prayers. That summer, I was fervently praying to sing again, to be used by the Lord again, and to do this thing I loved called "music."

Last year, God opened my eyes to see how those prayers played a significant role in my story. I'll explain further, but first, let me tell you that at the end of that month of vocal rest, my voice was healed and restored. I remember being so nervous the first weekend I was able to perform again. I discussed how I sounded with the vocal engineer, and his exact words were, "smooth like butter." I was healed. I could sing. Everything would be OK.

So, it was back to the weekly grind of rehearsals and services. Another kid's event was added to my plate. We had a Christian school where we turned our chapel service into a weekly family worship experience. I was in charge of leading a team of elementary students. I would teach them the worship songs and then choreograph motions to the songs. That spring, we also recorded what was the first "Little Praise Party" album. I wrote the music, and we made fun arrangements of some Sunday School classics to use in our preschool ministry.

I was meeting a need where kids could easily engage with the songs & curriculum. *Check.*

Write the songs, record, and perform them. *Check.*

Release the album. *Check.*

And then...

Everything in my world as I knew it completely shattered into pieces. It felt like every dream I had envisioned for my future was nothing more than a mere memory.

It was the worst, most painful ripping off of a band-aid ever. My season working at the church had come to an abrupt end. It was nothing I did. It wasn't my fault. The end of the chapter had already been written for me.

I always said that it was nothing I ever asked for, and that's the point where God spoke to me last year. He reminded me of the summer of 2006 and all the worship services where I'd lip sync in order to participate in worship. And, all those prayers I had lifted up. I realized it was nine months after my voice was restored that I was released into this season of ministry of leading, writing, and creating worship music for kids and families, along with resources for churches. *Nine*. The number of birthing. I *thought* the change was nothing I ever wanted or asked for. In the moment, I couldn't see it as an answer to prayer or a fulfillment of His promise, but that's exactly what this exodus had been about. It was to ultimately lead me to my promised land.

Within the next six months, I was completely certain my focus was kids + music. God made that crystal clear. By early 2008, I released "Rock-N-Happy Heart" an album geared for preteens. The rest is history. Later that year, we produced the first collection of "Little Praise Party" music videos. I didn't start with a great vision for what it could potentially be. I was simply just meeting needs. I tackled something for our church and it just happened to be something the Church, capital C, also needed.

Looking back now, I admit that I question myself and wonder, *"Why didn't we ever have the genius idea to mix my life history of children's ministry with my love and calling of music?"* None of us were that smart or clever. God knew all along, though. It was revealed one step at a time. Isn't that how He so often leads us? Let's be real, if He had told my 16-year-old self that my number one song on iTunes/

Apple Music one day would be a preschool song I wrote, I would have probably rolled my eyes. That wasn't my dream. That wasn't my end goal. I wasn't ready for the vision then. But I loved music, and in the years that followed, I would learn to write songs and record them. I would have the opportunity to travel to places in the world like Sweden, Australia, Romania, Canada, and Africa to sing my songs. Over time, every step and piece would become intertwined to tell a mosaic story of obedience.

That is my story that led me to this place where I live with a burning desire to help kids be the worshippers God created them to be. I have a vision for this generation to be discipled in their worship. I'm so glad you're here with me now. My heart is to share this vision I have, so the kids you lead and love can taste and see that He is good.

There is Power
in Kids Worship

Chapter Two

I can picture it all right now. I don't even have to close my eyes to go back to my office, even though it was many years ago. I can see the texture of the walls and the chair rail. I can look out the window that overlooked the front parking lot. The furniture was large and wooden. I'm sitting behind the desk, and a bookcase and my Wurlitzer electric piano sits to my left. I remember the day clearly, because of what the Lord downloaded in my spirit. It's so sweet when God's Word becomes tangible and alive with revelation to us. On that afternoon, I came across a scripture that I still hold dear. It's my motivation as a worship leader for kids. It's a bit of a promissory note from the Lord where He reveals to us what is at stake. He pulls the curtain back to show us what is happening in the spiritual world when children take part in worship.

Psalm 8:1-2 says, "God, brilliant Lord, yours is a household name. Nursing infants gurgle choruses about you; toddlers shout the songs that drown out enemy talk, and silence atheist babble." (MSG) I remember reading that verse and being gobsmacked by the truth that fills each line. I thought to myself, *read it again*, so, I did. I grabbed a post-it note, wrote out each word, and stuck it by my phone on the desk so that I'd see it over and over again throughout the day. This verse felt like a lifeline to me. It was an endorsement from God that what I was navigating by creating spaces for kids to engage in worship, mattered. And not just that it mattered, but that it was important. So often, we don't place enough value on what matters most in our lives. We focus our time and attention on things that are fleeting, while allowing the things that should be priorities to fade to the bottom of our never-ending to-do list. Then, we wonder why it's so easy to procrastinate and never actually do the thing we needed to do. Through the words of the Psalmist, I better understood what I was doing. My vision for kids worship began to form. My spirit began to see, *truly* see, for the first time.

I thought about friends that grew up in the church like I did. Friends that had similar family dynamics as mine. From the outside looking in, we had so much in common. However, in our adult lives, we've made very different choices. We grew up in the same environment, but we are not living according to the same convictions. It's heartbreaking. Some of these friends could even have an atheist label attached to their names. I remember grasping for the first time that even a group of snotty nosed two-year-olds, with all their varying temperaments and attitudes, singing the chorus of "How Great Is Our God," could make my friends stop in their tracks. It could inspire them to reconsider if maybe, just maybe, God is everything that I believe His Word tells us He is. This scripture gave me hope for the lost and the broken. It didn't reveal that the lost was going to experience the late Billy Graham deliver a remarkable message and be saved. It doesn't even say that if you sing songs from the CCLI Top 100 Worship Songs, then they will be saved. No. This verse talked about nursing infants gurgling choruses and toddlers shouting songs that would silence the enemy. Hallelujah!

The power of a toddler shouting songs that silence atheist babble is astounding. I was floored by that thought. How often have we overlooked a song time in one of our classrooms, not expecting it to really matter or mean that much? Yes, music serves us since it fills time slots while we wait for the class to be over and the parents to come pick up their kids. But, it's not about how many boxes we check off. How often are we consumed by how many minutes we need to creatively fill? I think most Kidmin leaders appreciate the wiggles that they can get out by using a song to make the whole room bounce up and down. How shortsighted have we been to think that's all it's about, though? For too long, we've had our eyes on the wrong thing. We've had the potential to have supernatural power at work in our classrooms, but we've sold it for a cheap counterfeit of an action song, instead. I am reminded of Jacob and Esau and how Esau sold his inheritance for a bowl of soup. How foolish! We've all judged his poor decision a time or two. It's ok to admit that. And yet, as I look at the landscape of children's ministry as a whole, I see how similarly we have sacrificed what could be for what we have, or what we think we need. How many times have we made decisions based on what we have chosen to believe are our shortcomings? You make a list of reasons for why you can't do it another way, or an excuse for why you can't lead a slow song. How many excuses were made because of our lack of personnel and team needs? We tend to focus on the short-term of surviving another Sunday. Is a bowl of soup bad? No, it isn't. We actually know that the soup can provide nourishment and sustain, but it's not eternal. It only provides what is needed temporarily. Esau didn't get an eternal bowl of porridge. He just got a meal. Jacob was the one who received the blessing. That's what I want, too. The blessing!

The Church is a storehouse for what should be life-giving and have eternal currency. How many times have we been guilty of giving the kids in our ministry a meal for the day or week ahead when what they needed to taste was the spirit of the Living God that will cause them to never hunger or thirst again?

I pictured our toddler classroom and received understanding that their worship matters to God. I grasped that the power that fills the melodies they sing could be so impactful that it affects those I know who have walked away from the church. I pictured families where the child is at church thanks to a parent, grandparent, or friend, but still has other family members who don't know Christ. These young children singing the chorus of a song they learned on a Sunday morning in your classroom, while they are in their room playing with toys or in the backyard climbing on a swing set, has the potential to affect that adult listening in. The presence of the Lord enters those homes and cars. It fills those backyards. That adult may not have been to church in decades, but the sound they hear as that child sings in worship to the Lord could forever alter the direction of their life. I truly believe the future of families is at stake here.

Although the scripture in the MSG translation speaks of the really young, I believe that the same is true regardless of the child's age. There is power in their worship. You may be struggling with fifth graders rolling their eyes at you. There is power in their worship. You may be leading kindergartners who can't read the words on the screen yet. There is power in their worship. You may find yourself teaching third graders whose legs get too tired to stand for the entire worship set. There is power in their worship. No child is excluded from this. Every single child of God, opening his or her mouth to declare the praises of the King, releases God's power to be at work and on the move.

I love how The Passion translation puts Psalm 8:2: "You have built a stronghold by the songs of babies. Strength rises up with the chorus of singing children. This kind of praise has the power to shut Satan's mouth. Childlike worship will silence the madness of those who oppose you." Yes! Amen and amen. Sign me up for a case of shutting Satan's mouth. Let's eliminate the lies of the devil. Let's loosen the grip of the enemy who's been at work distracting us from what really matters for far too long.

Please, hear me when I say this: There is power in kids worship. Every time you push play on a song, you are pressing play on God's power to be at work.

Every time you create a space for kids to experience the presence of the Lord, you are creating space for God's power to fill the atmosphere and penetrate hearts like only He can.

It's not just about doing songs. Songs in and of themselves aren't the goal here. Songs are part of the process and are important tools you have, but kids declaring the greatness of God as they give their praise and worship to the Lord is the goal.

When you become intentional about discipling kids to be the worshippers they were designed to be, then you unleash God's power to be fully and freely at work in your classrooms. I believe that then spills over into hallways and the gathering areas of your church. I believe it continues on into parking lots and the back seat of the family car. As kids share about what they learned and as they sing out the songs you were singing, even when they think no one is listening and can hear them, God's power is put on display in the earth. The presence of God can transform families. The future of your ministry looks bright, really bright, when you are looking at it through this lens of possibility.

Think of it like this. Imagine if I told you that there was a new, hot product that you could get for your church that would do exceedingly, abundantly more than you could imagine? It would increase discipleship. It would increase salvations. It would transform lives and bring miracle outcomes to situations. You'd probably be pretty intrigued, right? You may even ask me where to get it, and then willingly hand over your credit card. My friends, I'm telling you that there is something so good and so real that you have complete access to every single time you open the doors of your ministry. What if throughout the week, every time you gather and give care to kids by pressing play on a song, giving space for them to declare the greatness of who He is and what He has done, you put this resource into action? This amazing tool has been there since the beginning of time. God inhabits the praises of His people, remember? It has been right there waiting in the wings for us to wake up. Create the space and give time to prepare the way for His presence to be felt. After all, we know where two or three are gathered, He promises to be there.

Have you ever played the game "Hot and Cold?" You know, where you pick an object and give the player clues as to whether they are getting hotter or colder to the item? Are they moving closer or taking steps further away? When you know what the item is, but the other player is taking side steps, wrong turns, or making choices that lead them away from the chosen thing, it can make you feel crazy. You can see it. You know what it is, but somehow, they are still missing it. They are blinded to the answer.

My friend, may I invite you to consider what you've been searching for in your kids ministry? Come sit at the table where you'll discover what you knew you wanted, but were unable to describe in words. The place you have felt clueless of how to attain, or even how to get there, because you honestly weren't sure what this special place held. You're closer than you think. You are "hot, hot, hotter" to finding it with every word you read.

There is power in kids worship.

If you want them to experience the presence of God, then make time for it.

If you want them to sing about more than just fun and silly action songs, then stop only planning for those types of songs to be sung.

If you want them to learn how to worship God while they are children, and not when they are in college and thrust in the main adult service, then start being intentional in every area and age group to worship now.

When I took a closer look at Jacob and Esau, I noticed something in Hebrews 12:17. It says, "You know that afterward, when he wanted his father's blessing, he was rejected. It was too late for repentance, even though he begged with bitter tears." (NLT)

Can you imagine how crushed he was in that moment? He knew he had messed up. He was fully aware of the pain he had caused in his own life. He repented with bitter tears, yet the scripture says that he was rejected. Don't let it be said of us that we exchanged what could have been birthed in our kids if we had equipped them to be the worshippers God created them to be, all because we settled for some soup. I tremble at the thought of selling our kids short and reducing down opportunities for them to taste His goodness.

I truly believe in my heart of hearts that we will give an account for how we disciple kids in the area of worship. When we get to the pearly gates, the home of the streets of gold and diamond seas, we will be judged on how we helped these precious ones know who He is. May that be a sobering thought for many of us. As we reflect on recent weeks, months and years, may we evaluate and adjust our course.

For many of us this is a time for repentance. It's a line in the sand that we draw to say we will no longer sit back and waste these hours we have with children. I invite you to pray this prayer and repent because the Kingdom of God is at hand.

There is Power in Kids Worship

Dear God,

You are great and worthy to be praised.

I am so sorry for the opportunities I've missed to allow the kids I lead to sing Your praises and celebrate You. I repent for the times I programmed the wrong things to pass the time and fill the void. Reveal to me Your heart for worship. Guide my thoughts and plans to create space for You alone to be worshiped and magnified. I invite you to come, live, and move in us. Show me how to lead kids and point them to Your presence. You are the only thing that fills us up to overflowing. Help me as I lead kids to hunger and thirst for more of You, Jesus. May I lead by example. Oh, how I love You Jesus. Amen.

Hebrews 11 is considered to be "The Hall of Faith" chapter. One translation uses the headline, "Faith in Action," while another titles it, "The Power of Bold Faith." Reading through the chapter is like a Bible history lesson of those who wholeheartedly trusted and walked in obedience to the assignments which they had been called to. In verse 21, there is a beautiful picture of a characteristic of Christ followers that I want to encourage us not to overlook. "Jacob worshiped in faith's reality at the end of his life, and leaning upon his staff he imparted a prophetic blessing upon each of Joseph's sons." (TPT)

He worshiped in faith's reality at the end of his life. I love leading kids in worship. It is the very thing in which I've given my creative energy, time, and talents to. I don't write the songs I write and help kids learn about worship because I'm focused on where they are right now. I know that life will be just that: life. It will likely hand them some lemons. It will throw a bruise or a cut their way. They may try to carry a burden that was never theirs to bear. They don't stay children forever. They become mothers and fathers, aunts and uncles, and grandparents who will proclaim from one generation to another what He has done! I am focused on who they will become. I'm sharpening my arrows to go where I guide them. I am equipping them for the battles of life that, through Jesus, they will overcome and see victory. Every child becomes an adult. I'm not as focused on leading kids in worship as I am on raising disciples who know what they were created to do, and who understand the power that their worship yields.

May we say in faith that the kids we lead will "worship in faith's reality at the end of their lives." May we train them up in the way they should go. May we create space and room for God's presence to be felt in our classrooms so that they can't wait to come back through the doors to taste it some more. Again and again and again. May our kids grow into adults who have their own kids, passing on a godly heritage and example of obedience and faith to the future generations of their families.

What you do isn't just about Sunday. It's about their future.

There is power in their worship.

Let's disciple them to know how to use that power well.

The Devil Went Down to...Church

Last year, I was recording a podcast interview on the topic of worship. Unlike most podcasts via phone or Zoom, it was actually an in-person interview where I was sitting across the table from my interviewer. Toward the end of our conversation, he said something off the cuff about "worship being a lifestyle," and immediately saw the look on my face. I'm one of those people that can't easily hide the expressions on my face. I clearly revealed my opposing thoughts. He kindly opened the discussion up for me to unpack the struck nerve he had just hit.

First, let me begin by saying that I fully agree. Worship *is* a lifestyle. That is a completely true statement. Worship is more than the songs we sing. The issue I have is, in most cases, I hear the statement expressed by a pastor or leader who is using it as an excuse. It has become a bandage for a wound that we haven't allowed to heal. It's become a crutch of the modern church that is built on a shifting foundation. Well-meaning, God fearing leaders express a comment like that as if it's a singular statement. However, worship can't be your lifestyle only when the conditions surrounding worship meet *your* expectations. Whether it's the right song, the volume level is perfect, and there aren't too many moving lights, or it's a grandeur room with stained glass, the hymnal pages are turned, and the voices are acapella. Maybe you have quantified your worship participation based on your preferred leader on stage. We all have our favorites, right? Worship isn't about the right person leading. Worship isn't about the song of the moment being sung. Even writing out the reasons that we've all heard churchgoing believers say, sounds ridiculous. They sound so much about us. When did we become so pompous? Worship isn't about us, it's about the Holy One. Our worship is a response to who He is.

The reason alarms and sirens go off in my spirit every time I hear *"Worship is a lifestyle,"* is because it's a conditional statement. Worship is *not* conditional. It is not "instead of." It is not an either/ or scenario. As a Christ follower, there is not an option to opt-out of worship. In most cases, I hear the phrase used in a sweeping under the rug manner. As in, *"Don't feel bad that you come late to church so you can skip the songs being sung. Don't feel guilty that you're not engaging in the music set, or lifting your hands. You're not less of a Christian because, never fear, worship is just a lifestyle."* That statement should not give you the freedom to justify your lack of participation in a worship service. That statement is not a "get out of jail free" card that allows you to stand and simply watch worship happen around you on Sunday morning, or exclude it from the other days of the week. People say that phrase as if it's a badge of honor to wear: "Well, I don't have to participate in worship because my life is an offering of worship." It's no blue ribbon prize, friends. It doesn't eradicate the scriptures in God's Word that talk about our singing of praise and our bowing down to honor the Lord. Our musical expression of worship matters.

When I hear pastors and leaders express this sentiment, in most cases it's because they don't value the musical portion of worship. They may not be "music people." I've known many pastors like this. In my experience, they have not had their eyes awakened to the truth of what is at stake when we don't disciple people and nurture their spirits to grow and develop in worship. There are great churches who are discipling people to do great and mighty things. Giving in missions to spread the gospel around the globe is important. Loving one another is important. Showing kindness to my neighbor and being the hands and feet of Jesus to the orphan and the widow are all very real and needed aspects of being a Christ follower. We have people who have responded and received the grace and mercy of Jesus, but have not learned how to bow at His feet and give Him honor. It's the same as receiving a birthday gift from a family member or friend, taking the gift, but never pausing to express gratitude for that gift.

I am someone who appreciates thank you notes. I'm a stationary-loving girl. Nothing makes me feel more seen than receiving a card in the mail from someone that my life impacted. It also brings me great joy and delight to pull out my stationary and write a sentiment of thanks for a gift. Maybe it was kindness expressed, but to pause and put into words what the expression meant to me is an important task in my day.

Likewise, I adore giving gifts. Wrapping presents is truly one of the most relaxing things to me. I'm very much against gift bags. If you ever receive a gift in a bag from me, then you know I didn't have time to prepare and was throwing it in a bag with some tissue, as I quickly walked out the door. I cringe just at the thought, but once in a while have been there. Of course, I realize this is the very reason y'all love them. They are quick. But, let's be real. It's hard to have an exciting ending with a gift from a bag. The gift is revealed quickly. On the flipside, the wrapped present is the complete opposite. It takes more time & effort to wrap and disguise the gift. The final execution can be a lovely presentation of paper, ribbons, and trim. And, unwrapping the gift takes more time, especially if you're one of those neat unwrappers who doesn't like ripping the paper. There's a bigger expectation as the gift is slowly being revealed. When my oldest son was little, he would yell out, "secret box!," anytime he unwrapped a gift that had a generic box and he couldn't see what was inside yet. More waiting, more expectation. When the gift is finally revealed, the level of excitement and wonder is higher. I think there's a connection between my love for worship, thank you notes, and wrapped presents.

Our worship is very much a "thank you note" to God. It's our response to what He has done, and the work He's currently doing in our lives. Just as you take joy in receiving a note from someone thanking you for a gift or a job well-done, God loves it when we take delight in what He has done for us. When we take the time to express our heart of thanks, it moves the heart of God.

We don't have to pay Jesus for the life that He has freely given us. He's not holding it against us that He died on the cross for us. That was a gift that He so bravely and generously gave us. It's a love like we've never known before. We were given a gift, and the gift we can give in return, is every ounce of our lives. Every breath in our lungs and task on our to-do list are His. When I look across a sanctuary full of believers and see a lack of expression as they are invited to take part in worship, which is often similar to prayers that we sing, my heart breaks. Every single part of our lives are full of responses and expressions. When we are moved, we respond. This is true in our relationships, at our jobs, moments with our family and friends, when we are watching our favorite team play, and the list goes on. It is in our nature to be expressive human beings. Every single person has that "thing" that makes them light up, do a happy dance, and get overly excited.

When we truly grasp how priceless the gift we've received truly is, how could we not respond with something that costs us? Our worship is costly. At times, it is a sacrifice. It's not always what we *feel* in the initial moment. But, I've never come to the end of worship and thought, "Man, I wish I had participated less." I cringe at that thought. How often do you analyze the end of a service by whether or not they sang all your favorite songs, or question what you didn't care for? Have you been guilty of evaluating all the wrong things rather than asking, "How was my offering of worship today? Did I hold anything back from the King?"

As leaders, it's easy to downplay the weight and cost of our worship when it equates to one less thing we have to deal with. I get it. The ministry of the church requires much. There are many who are stretched thin. There's only so much time and only so many people ready to serve. The lies we tell ourselves about worship is more to self-serve our tasks and goals for the quarter. We allow ourselves to continue sliding by because it's easier than investing time into prayer and vision, recruiting and training, and seeking the Lord over the songs we should introduce and lead. Begin by interceding for your kids. Pray that they will take the necessary steps to fall more in love with the King. I believe we've sacrificed kids experiencing the presence of God, while going through the motions of singing worship songs, for far too long.

We are in the middle of a battle. This battle isn't about flesh and blood. It is in the spirit realm. I was fortunate to know country legend, Charlie Daniels. We were a part of the same church for a season. I even had the privilege of singing on stage with him once. An incredibly kind, talented, and Jesus-fearing man. Charlie is known for his classic, "The Devil Went Down to Georgia." It's a song that tells a story. The Devil battling against this talented fiddle player, vying to be the winner of his soul. Maybe you're a visual learner and imagining the scene of this song helps you picture what is taking place. For far too long, Christians have been naïve to think that a battle for our attention hasn't been at play.

Satan is in the business of distracting believers. One of his choice plots is dangling carrots over here and ringing shiny bells over there so that we ultimately lose focus. In the garden of Eden, he used an apple. It was proof that our sinful nature will sacrifice a lot for a measly piece of fruit dipped in lies. The Devil wants us to become more, while God becomes less, but we know that's the wrong equation. He's in the business of putting blinders on our eyes so the holiness of the Lord becomes harder to recognize.

Many theologians believe Lucifer was a worship leader in Heaven. Although we aren't fully certain of that, we do know that he is a fallen angel. Do you know what the angels do? The same thing they've done since the beginning of time. The same thing that they will be doing for eternity and beyond: worshiping. Angels are singing a continuous song of praise that has been sung and will be sung, forevermore.

"Holy, holy, holy is the Lord God, the Almighty—the one who always was, who is, and who is still to come. Whenever the living beings give glory and honor and thanks to the one sitting on the throne (the one who lives forever and ever), the twenty-four elders fall down and worship the one sitting on the throne (the one who lives forever and ever). And they lay their crowns before the throne and say, "You are worthy, O Lord our God, to receive glory and honor and power. For you created all things, and they exist because you created what you pleased." (Revelations 4:8-11)

"Holy, holy, holy." Always three, because He is the trinity.

"Holy, holy, holy," because He is the same yesterday, today, and

forever.

I've been guilty of joking that many Christians are going to be disappointed by heaven. It's a non-stop worship party there. I personally think the streets of gold are a sparkling and glam-loving dream to anticipate. Our time on earth and the worship services we attend on Sunday mornings are all a rehearsal for eternity. I might sound funny saying these things, but I'm sincere. Worship is a part of *Who* and *what* we are created for. Our time on earth matters. What songs do I want to be found singing and proclaiming? What is the posture I want displayed in my body and in my countenance?

In Revelations, we are reminded of the throne at the center of it all. It's the place where the revelation song is being sung. It's been sung from the beginning of time and it never stops. We are just periodically joining into the song that's already being played in the heavenlies.

"Then I looked again, and I heard the voices of thousands and millions of angels around the throne and of the living beings and the elders. And they sang in a mighty chorus: 'Worthy is the Lamb who was slaughtered— to receive power and riches and wisdom and strength and honor and glory and blessing.' And then I heard every creature in heaven and on earth and under the earth and in the sea. They sang: 'Blessing and honor and glory and power belong to the one sitting on the throne and to the Lamb forever and ever.'" (Revelations 5:11-13)

I heard a powerful sermon that I would highly recommend downloading. Darrell Johnson shared a message entitled, "Something Changed in Heaven." It's unlike anything I've ever heard. When I had the fortunate opportunity to meet him after a conference he was speaking at, I commented on how impressed I was that I had never heard anyone share what he taught us. His humble response was, "It's in the Bible." How many times are we, as believers, guilty of missing information that's been right under our nose the entire time?

One of the biggest areas of division in the church is over the music.

When I think about the divide over what our worship should sound like and how it should look, it grieves my heart. We have churches arguing about the number of verses in a song, and even what key the song should be sung in. I can't help but believe that we've missed the mark for far too long. When I think about pastors who have lied to themselves and their flock by emphasizing worship as a lifestyle, while minimizing the power of worship music, it makes me incredibly sad. Your life can be full of acts *of* worship, but if you haven't learned how to sing and bow *in* worship, then you're only partially experiencing true consecration unto the Lord. You see, the devil knows the power of our worship. He knows about it because he's experienced it. He knows because he's been a part of the hallelujah chorus and probably even struck up the band for the hymn of the day. He's experienced the power of the throne and the song of holies being sung. He is aware of the power that it holds. I am convinced that he uses this place of tension within the church to distract us from the very thing we should be focused on.

But, make no mistake, we are also talking about the person who is silenced by the name of Jesus. The one who fell from heaven. Satan cowards down when we pray in the name of Jesus *and* when we glorify His name in worship. Has the devil been vying to distract our attention away from the throne for far too long? A resounding *YES*. I truly believe he has. Will you allow him to get the last word? What do you need to shift and change in your own life in order to ensure that the victory that is ours will be proclaimed? How will you personally give thanks unto the Lord and proclaim that He is good so others will hear the word of your testimony and be moved by His presence?

He dwells in our praise. The Word tells us that the Lord inhabits the praises of His people (Psalm 22:3, KJV). It's time to stop devaluing the power of our worship, both in our personal lives and within the four walls of our churches.

Lucifer has been doing everything he can to keep us from singing. Even in recent times, and in certain places, music and singing have been considered unsafe. Can you see the attack for what it is? The devil wants to silence us and our praises. Let's draw a line in the sand and stop making excuses as to why our worship isn't vital. We've become lawyers writing clauses into a contract so that we can get our way, but in reality, the agreement was signed long before. You can justify your actions with every excuse that has blinded you, but it doesn't change the actual truth.

It is by no accident that in the original Hebrew text of the Bible, one of the many words for praise is **Zamar** ("zaw-mar"). It means, "to make music; to celebrate joyfully in song; to pluck the strings or parts of a musical instrument."

Zamar is a musical word. According to scripture, giving praise to God is *musical*. Yes, we offer worship to God with our lives and the various choices we make, but there is something special that happens when an instrument is played, when a sound or a rhythm is expressed, and when the voice of creation sings to give praise and honor to the Creator of all things. We were made to worship God and give Him our praise, just like every bird that sings and every wave that crashes in the ocean proclaims the greatness of God.

Have you ever been moved by a song? It could have been at a concert, a school performance, at church, or while watching a movie.

It could have been the band, the words being sung, or the heart being expressed. Has music ever made the hairs on your arms stand up? At times, music can bring us to tears when we connect to it on a deeper level. It can stir feelings and can help us verbalize the thoughts in our hearts that we wouldn't be able to put into words without the help of that one song.

Psalm 57:7 says, "God, my heart feels secure. My heart feels secure. I will sing and make music to you."

God understands that music is a gift because He created it. He knows that there is power in music, whether it's played on an instrument or sung with a voice. Praising God with Zamar can give us the feelings and the words we need to declare, proclaim, and give our worship to the ONLY One in our lives that truly deserves it. Praising God with Zamar commands us to sing and make music. You can only learn to worship by worshiping.

Our musical act of worship has been overlooked and neglected. Praise and worship without music is void of what it was originally intended for. Let's fall to our knees and do the intensive heart work needed in order to make worship more than just a lifestyle.

Can we worship with our lives? Absolutely. But, the tension will remain because you can't remove music and song from worship and expect that it will be whole. They are crucial parts to the equation. It's not a choice between two things, or "instead of" something else. You have to have ALL the parts in order for worship to be whole, complete, and be as it was intended.

Chapter Four

Man After
God's Own Heart

I'm not ashamed to admit that I am a total fangirl of David in the Bible. He gives us the purest picture of worship of any other Bible character. David certainly had some greatest hits in his time. After all, he's the boy who killed the giant. He's the youngest brother who was anointed king, in spite of being unexpectedly chosen. He wasn't even invited to the selection process. He worked in the field to shepherd and tend the flock. He was left in the middle of the pasture to get the work done for that day. If that happened in the majority of our modern families, there would undoubtedly be hurt feelings. Fingers would be pointed, blame would be cast, and grudges would grow. Identities would be broken and defeated. In this generation of offense, any rule that discriminates is looked at as a personal attack rather than a guideline for how a business chooses to run. David's family situation may have made them candidates for a daytime talk show that highlights family drama and discourse. His own father didn't believe there was any chance that the young one would be chosen. And yet, right in the middle of David's story, we see so much of the gospel on display for us. How much of God's perfect plan for our lives do we miss because of the limitations we place on ourselves? When we compare and when we believe lies said about who we are and what we're capable of, we extinguish the plans that God had for us before our first breath was taken.

We all know David didn't live a perfect life. On that note, he wasn't much different than any of us. Yet, God used David in a mighty way. This should give us great hope. God is a God who cares about the posture of our hearts, first and foremost. 1 Samuel 16:7 says, "For the Lord sees not as man sees: man looks on the outward appearance, but the Lord looks on the heart."(ESV) In the eyes of many, David was just a shepherd boy. To others, he was a man who sinned greatly against the Lord. He had committed adultery and murder. His past wasn't exactly a shining star on a Sunday School bulletin board. And while he was a man who was deeply familiar with his sin, he was also a repentant man who longed to dwell in the house of the Lord and offer his life as worship to His King. He was a man after God's own heart. And because of that desire, God was able to use him where others might have written him off.

David was given the title, "A man after God's own heart," by God himself. It's a description that is uniquely his, and one that has become the desire of my heart. That those we lead would be boys and girls, men and women after God's own heart. I believe that David was given that title because he understood something not all believers do. He worshiped God. Period. It wasn't conditional. There was no "and, if, but, or why," about it. He didn't have to have the perfect situation or a time set on his calendar. He didn't just worship on the mountaintops or on special holidays. David worshiped God. That was a period. Mic drop. End of story. Worship was a defining characteristic of his life and the view of his life that was ordained by God to be displayed in His Word for you and me.

David found his strength in the presence of the Lord. He used the songs he sang to declare what was true about God. I don't believe that David only sang about the "fortress and hiding place" of God after he had personally seen the evidence on display in his own life. David spoke out and prophesied into his reality and declared that God is a rock, a shelter, and a hiding place when he was likely in need of that very truth in his life.

David was a man after God's heart *because* of His worship. It was the secret place where he drew close to the Father. It was where he sacrificed his trust, believing that God was the answer. This is a gift that you can give to the kids in your ministry, by helping them find their refuge and sense of belonging in God's presence.

One of my favorite verses in the Bible is found in Jeremiah 29:13. It says, "You will seek me and find me when you seek me with all your heart." That's an invitation for us, but it's also a guarantee. I love that we have this promise that when we seek God, we will find Him. Worship is the ticket we have to get us in the door to find God's presence. David understood this action of seeking the Lord. That one discipline better prepared him for the greater things that God had in store for his life.

David was anointed king, but he still went into a season of waiting and preparing for the chosen time. He didn't just land there overnight.

David bravely faced Goliath and, by faith, threw those rocks that defeated the giant. Never underestimate what a foundation that can't be shaken, mixed with faith in action, looks like, right!? On the actual battlefield, David developed and persevered in his faith to fight the spiritual battles he would face. However, I'd venture to say that it was his posture in worship that ultimately prepared him for those battles that took place in the natural.

I have spent a decent amount of time looking at David's life and learning from him. Throughout the *Heartbeat* curriculum series that I developed with my friend, Johnny Rogers, we focus on helping you teach kids the heart of worship. David was our focus for every Bible story we explored and taught, so we would be better equipped to help kids learn the attributes and action steps of developing a heart after God.

I recently hopped on Facebook, as we often do throughout the day, and saw a post by a friend I grew up with. It was someone who had interned with my dad and later became a children's pastor himself. This particular post was to update their family and friends on some news. They had found out they were unexpectedly pregnant with another child. They worked through their shock and found the delight of their family expanding. However, before many had found out about the news, they experienced another element of shock. They lost the baby. You may be able to identify with their story. There are many who find themselves having to work through the pain, heartbreak, and loss of a child. I've been there myself.

As my friend continued with his story, he shared that the same day they received news of their loss, he had been studying the life of David. He had taken solace and direction from this verse in 2 Samuel 12:19-20 that says: "David noticed that his attendants were whispering among themselves, and he realized the child was dead. "Is the child dead?" he asked. "Yes," they replied, "he is dead." Then David got up from the ground. After he had washed, put on lotions, and changed his clothes, he went into the house of the Lord and worshiped."

Did you catch that? David's child had *died* and scripture says his response was to get up, wash his face, change his clothes, and then go to church and *worship*. It doesn't say that he fell apart in anguish, although it's hard to imagine how he wouldn't. It doesn't say he stayed in bed for three days and didn't go to work. The story isn't that he hopped on his smartphone and wrote a sad post to share the news with everyone who he had ever known. It doesn't say he ate his feelings away with pizza and ice cream. No, scripture tells us that his reaction was to worship. If we only referenced this one story in David's life, it would be evidence enough for the point that I'm trying to share with you. **David worshiped God. The end.**

THIS is why he was the one known as the man after God's heart.

If you didn't take anything else to heart in this book except that one thing, your life as a Christ follower would be changed forever. The strength of your faith would grow stronger. The story your life tells would proclaim the truth louder and more boldly. The things that you hunger and thirst for would be straight from the heart of the Father. To be known and to know more fully how good His providence and presence truly is. You would encourage and refresh your spirit, because times of refreshing come from being in the presence of the Lord. The hope that you're so often seeking would become new mercies for every day. I believe you would become more like Jesus simply because of time spent drawing near and experiencing His nature.

Chapter Five

The Picture of a
Worship Leader

If we want instruction from scripture on what being a worship leader looks like, David's example is a no brainer. I believe there is so much we can learn from not only looking at David's example of how he modeled praise and worship, but also the words he wrote as instruction. Scripture tells us that out of the abundance of the heart the mouth speaks (Luke 6:45, ESV). When I opened my Bible to learn about leading worship from David, here were my main takeaways:

First, David taught us that worship matters. Everything on earth worships God.

"Everything on earth will worship you; they will sing your praises, shouting your name in glorious songs." (Psalm 66:4)

Everything does not leave anyone out. It includes everything. No exceptions or excuses made. We were made to worship the Lord our God. Humans were made for the glory of God. Isaiah 43:7 says, "everyone who is called by my name, whom I created for my glory, whom I formed and made." I challenge you to start making time in your class to worship. The games you play are fun. They have a place and a purpose. They are a tool to reach kids, but they do not matter in the way that your time of worship as a class matters. Can you do all things for the glory of God? Yes, I believe you can! However, there is no replacement for our response as a child of God to a loving Heavenly Father than our worship to Him. He *delights* in your worship. Let that sink in. Scripture even tells us that He is singing over us. (Zephaniah 3:17)

It's crucial that we STOP just *doing* songs and START *leading* worship. Worship is more than activity songs and time fillers. Worship is a response that we give to God for who He is and how He has changed our lives. I love this quote from C.S. Lewis: "The task of the modern educator is not to cut down jungles, but to irrigate deserts." Let's irrigate deserts in the lives of those we lead so they can pour out their love on the One who is always faithful. Help them flourish and bloom by giving glory to God through their worship.

Never forget that there is power in worship, especially when kids worship with their whole hearts. Let me remind you of where we began in Psalm 8:1-2. Pause now and read it again if you need to be reminded of the power that is found in the sound of kids surrendering their worship. There is nothing in this world like it! There is absolutely no replacement for it. Their worship is ordained by God. It matters!

If we travel through the Psalms, we see that David did three key things: Lead, teach, and model worship. So, we should be able to follow this example. Pushing play on a video does not lead worship for you. Videos are a tool we have. They are great. I make them. I sell them. I use them. But, there is no perfect video that is going to lead worship *for* you. There. I said it. You can't expect a video to lead your time of worship. You or another member of your team must teach and model worship in order to effectively lead the time of worship. What happens when we are watching a video at home or when we are killing time on our smartphone? We *watch* the video. We don't hop up and mimic everything we are watching. The same is true for the kids you lead. Simply watching it does not guarantee that they are going to follow along and mirror what they see. They need someone to lead them. You need to navigate and lead the worship time, and invite them to participate. It may just be you. It may be another volunteer. You may have an entire team doing this, while developing a kids worship team along with it. No matter how big or small your team may be, your kids need someone to lead them through worship.

I truly pray this next statement will be an encouragement to you. **Leading worship is more about your leadership ability than your musical ability.** Let me say that again: Leading worship is more about your leadership ability than your musical ability. The same qualities that make a great worship leader, a great worship leader, are the same qualities that make any great teacher, a great teacher. It's the same as the person on your team who is a great communicator and has the audience captivated by their every word. It requires having awareness of who you are speaking to. Knowing how to relate to them in a way that peaks their interest so they will look to you as an authority on the topic. And, if you realize it may not be clicking, it will mean that you'll need to figure out another way of explaining, so they will fully grasp the concepts. The qualities that make me a successful worship leader have very little to do with my ability to sing on pitch, or even count to four or three or six. (If you are musical, then you'll understand what I just said, but even if you aren't, it doesn't matter.) I'm not saying that it's okay for the person leading worship to be tone deaf. If you know your voice sounds like nails on a chalkboard, then please spare us all and don't try singing into a microphone. That's the blessing of kids worship. You can rely on the voices on the recording you're using. So, you may need to pull your mic away during the singing sections, but do you know what you can do instead? Introduce the song. Be aware of the arrangement of the song so you can insert a "Sing that again" or "Sing it louder this time." You can lead others on what to do during the instrumental of the song and transition between songs. To "lead worship" means more than just standing on stage and singing songs.

We're pretty familiar with the title of "worship leader." So, let's take a look at the word "leader." I love looking up definitions of words in the dictionary. I'll never forget looking up the word "leader" and being shocked by its simple definition: "A person or thing that leads." It seemed so simple that it felt uncalled for and pointless that I had taken the time to check it's meaning. But a worship leader, by definition, means "a person that leads worship." If you're leading worship and no one is joining in with you, may I submit that you're just a "worship singer" and not a "worship leader?"

I want to share a picture of what I believe our role as worship leaders is supposed to look like. Have you ever found what you thought was going to be an awesome workout program? Maybe it was something being shared online. It likely had a big promise of the type of results you could achieve with a not-so-big commitment. You jumped and thought, "This is what I've been looking for!" So, you head to a gym alone, prepared to give this new workout your very best. Maybe you even bought new yoga pants or tennis shoes for the occasion, because you thought it would help motivate you even more. So, on that first day at the gym, you start doing the exercises you're supposed to do. Everything is off to a good start...until you get to one particular exercise that proves to be a bit more challenging. You're supposed to do three sets of twenty reps, but instead, you make it to the second set and rep twelve, and it all starts falling apart. You're now feeling the burn. Let's admit, it hurts a bit. Things are getting hard and you're wondering how you can make it stop and just quit right there. But you're not a quitter, so you give it your very best and push through to the end of that set. Then you stop for a water break that extends into a pause for a social media check, that then turns into a few quick responses to emails. Before you know it, you've convinced yourself that it was a great first day, even though you left the gym without completing the full list of exercises. You're now racing down the street to your favorite coffee shop for a treat. Some of you are laughing right now because you know it's true. It's safe to admit that most of us, when left to ourselves, are not motivated enough to hit our workout goals. So, let's adjust the situation a bit.

Have you ever worked out with a personal trainer or taken a cardio class? Maybe you grew up playing sports in school and had a coach who made you run way too many laps or complete a list of things that weren't easy, and likely at a time when you wished you were still sleeping. In my lifetime, I've worked out with a personal trainer in seasons. I currently take workout classes several times a week, where the instructor is saying words that motivate and encourage me to keep going. It's almost as if they can sense when the mindset to quit and pause is creeping in my brain. Then, they'll say something that will challenge and remind me that I am stronger than I think. I can keep pushing and make it a few more reps to ten. That trainer has stood next to me when I didn't think I could push another bar of weights up, and told me that, in fact, I could. He counted it down. He cheered me on. He helped me say "yes" to this challenge of exercise that was only going to make my physical body in better shape than when I first began. The workout helps me maintain my body (aka: the temple of the Lord). I struggle to stay motivated on my own. But, it's amazing what happens when I book classes that have financial expense attached, and I show up and listen to the teacher's words wash over me, even when I feel like I can't do it. They tell me that I can. With their help, I'm able to accomplish far more in my health goals than I ever could on my own.

To me, this is the perfect picture of what our job as a worship leader looks like.

I refuse to believe that the majority of your kids are showing up to church and planning a way to spite you or refuse to engage in worship during service. I mean, there might be that one kid who is plotting a way to bring pain and suffering to you, but I digress. Let's not worry about that troublemaker who shall remain nameless. I honestly think the majority of your group would say that they desire to participate in the worship time. Then what happens, aside from their lack of understanding and knowledge of what the time is about? I'll tell you what happens. You're only one minute into the first song when a fly crosses their line of sight, they get distracted, and have now stopped singing because they are busy watching this fly land on ten kids' heads in the rows in front of them. For another, their stomach growls, which makes them think about lunch and their family's favorite restaurant that they are going to after church. Or, it could be a couple kids in the row behind them who are talking to each other and it's just loud enough that it's a distraction. They turn to see what's going on behind them, which makes them disengage from you leading them in worship. Before you know it, these kids are no longer participating. What you said before the song has completely escaped their mind and focus. If you never say anything in the song again, then you'll never get their attention. If you don't segue between songs or say something to inspire and motivate them before the third song, then they will never resume with what you're wanting to bring their focus back to.

Think of how many times you have to ask your children or spouse to do something before they pay attention and follow through with action. Your continuous coaching and encouragement is needed. I would even say that it's a necessity. By reminding them to "sing this from your heart," or saying, "everybody sing it loud this time," you've re-invited them to join in the worship that is happening. You're regaining their attention and realigning their focus to be on God, instead of on the fly, the distraction behind them, or in their own stomach. It's the same as that coach or aerobics instructor who is saying specific words that motivate and challenge you to keep going. As worship leaders, it's important that we insert those timely reminders, invitations, and commands so those we lead will get the spiritual workout they need during worship, instead of holding back our hearts, affection, time, or physical responses. Let's encourage those we lead to give it all to God. We get to prepare the table for their sacrifice of praise to be surrendered.

Kids are used to being told what to do. They receive instruction from parents, teachers, and coaches. They are receiving instruction from you in other areas while at church. If we truly believe that our worship matters, and if we are aware of the power that is within the sound of their worship, then now is the time to guide them on what to do and how to do it during worship, as well. You are their trainer and coach preparing them for a life of devotion to the Lord. We trust the exercise instructor or coach who is helping us workout in order to grow and develop our physical bodies. The process of the training actually helps us become healthier and stronger. Worship leaders are also instructors and coaches who are helping people grow and develop spiritually. Let's help kids become healthy and strong by teaching, modeling, and leading them to the type of worship God is seeking.

My longtime friend, Josh Blount, once shared a valuable piece of wisdom. He said, "Teaching kids to worship is not the issue. They know how to. Directing their worship to Jesus is the issue. Help them to put God first." That is what worship is all about. Surrendering and laying down all we are to lift Jesus up to the place of honor and glory that only He deserves.

The Invitation

Chapter Six

The second takeaway we can learn from David's example of leading worship is the invitation he extends. He didn't just worship alone; he summoned others to join in with him.

David teaches us how to participate and invites us to do so as well.

I love this scripture in Psalm 47:1 that says, "Come, everyone! Clap your hands! Shout to God with joyful praise!" It's not one of the longest verses in the Bible. It's pretty short, actually. However, inside this little verse are four pieces of instruction from David to you, me, and every believer that has come before us, and will come after us. In this verse David said:

1. *Come, everyone!*
2. *Clap your hands!*
3. *Shout to God!*
4. *With joyful praise!*

I believe David is giving us a perfect example of how we should be leading and inviting others to join into worship. David told us exactly what to do and how to do it.

Several years back, I was getting ready to speak at a conference. I ended up with a few extra minutes in my hotel room, so I did what we often do when killing time: I hopped on social media. Immediately, I saw a status update by someone I knew. If I said his name, you'd probably recognize it. He had songs on Christian radio in the past, and was nominated for a Best New Artist Dove Award at one point. This friend's status said, "I don't want to be a cheerleader of worship. I want my worship to inspire the audience I lead." Although I have no doubt my friend meant well, my blood pressure began to skyrocket thinking about his statement. Does that ever happen to you on social media? Please know I share this story with all judgment in my voice included. Can you hear it?

I've read articles about similar things. In adult worship circles, I know for a fact that there's an ongoing position and debate to not demand much from the crowd. Don't hype them up. Just worship and watch everyone in the room follow your example, much like a game of dominoes. And while I do believe our example is important, it's not the only piece of the equation here. I've been to far too many churches where I look around the room while being led in worship, and I don't see people engaged. I understand that there are some worshiping who don't appear to be. I'm not speaking to those exceptions here. I am speaking to the devoted Christ follower who thinks their worship is conditional. That it's based on being in the right place, with the most talented leader on stage, and their favorite song being sung, or that another expression of worship can take the place of the musical one. There are too many scriptures about the musical form of worship that we cannot ignore. We already talked about that in chapter three. It's never "instead of," but always, "in addition to." Worship is our response to the Lord, but when people are more comfortable looking like frozen statues who are unmoved by the power of the cross, I can't help but question if the people in the room really comprehend the love of the Father and the miracle of the resurrection. Because when you've been in a low valley where the way out seems to be nonexistent, and where all you can do is cry out to the Lord for help because you know there's no way out in your own strength, then it will motivate you to not only stand in worship, but to extend your hands and sing words that belt out the praises of the One who delivered you from the miry clay. You'll want to pour your heart out to the One who set your feet upon the rock, because you can now boast confidently that your hope is in the Lord, alone. We have far too many churches that look like they are only moments away from allowing the rocks to cry out in their place. Well, not on my watch. Not in my sphere of influence. Not in the rooms where I get the beautiful responsibility to stand and be the director of the choir of saints to sing and bless the Lord.

While I was still worked up, it was time for me to leave my hotel room and walk next door to the convention center where I was teaching a breakout session. As I walked, I duked it out with God. Do you ever do that? I cried out, "Why did he say that? Why do worship leaders have that stance on leading worship!?" God can handle your questions. He can handle your high blood pressure and He can calm your frustrations about someone else. Let it out and let it go. The Bible says in James 4:5, "If any of you lacks wisdom, you should ask God, who gives generously to all without finding fault, and it will be given to you." Ask Him for wisdom and allow God, through His Holy Spirit, to speak to you. He is our helper, so allow Him to help. So, after my questions, I felt God tell me to look at David. How did David model leading worship? After all, He is the worship leader that is leading us through those powerful and, oftentimes, famous Psalms. (Think about Psalm 23, 40, and 103, just to name a few. I mean, David definitely has a greatest hits album that's been on the charts longer than any artist I know of.) We see David inserting instruction. He doesn't just show us worship; he invites us to join in with the praises of our God.

The Invitation

Take another look at Psalm 47:1. In the KJV, it says to "shout unto God with a voice of triumph." Then, in Psalm 134:2 we're told to "Lift up your hands in the sanctuary and praise the Lord." (Emphasis mine.)

In Psalm 13:6, he models "follow me as I follow Christ" when he says, "I will sing the Lord's praise, for he has been good to me." And again in Psalm 16:5,9 when he proclaims, "Lord, you alone are my portion and my cup; you make my lot secure. Therefore my heart is glad and my tongue rejoices; my body also will rest secure."

He also testified of God's deliverance in Psalm 18.

So, what's your story? How have you seen God move in your life? What's the reason you have to worship? We all learn by story. The light bulb moment for some will be hearing you, as their leader, share how you know God is true and worthy of praise. When you have something about your story that connects to a song, then share that in your set-up and introduction. Pour your heart out and model how, even in the midst of a battle, your song of praise is a safe place to wage war against the enemy. It is the battleground where we see victory. My pastor, Henry Seeley, says it like this: "Praise precedes the miracle."

There are those who you lead that need to hear how precious God is, more precious than any material possession we could seek to acquire. Look how David beautifully articulated how important God's commands are in Psalm 19:10: "They are more precious than gold, than much pure gold; they are sweeter than honey, than honey from the honeycomb." His description gives us a visual of the value and weight of the Lord's laws.

Others will have their "aha" moment as you engage their senses to imagine the sweetness that's greater than the most perfect local, raw honey they've ever tasted on their tongues. Words communicate. They illustrate things that pull on your heart strings and make you feel, or suddenly understand, more clearly than you have before.

Let's take a look at all the action words David led people to take. He wasn't simply allowing them to watch him worship; he was summoning them to worship the living God. David gave instruction to the faithful people of God to **SING** in Psalm 30:4 when he says, "Sing the praises of the Lord, you his faithful people; praise his holy name."

In Psalm 31:23-24, he admonishes us to "Love the Lord....Be strong and take heart."

In Psalm 32:11, he tells us to "Rejoice in the Lord and be glad, you righteous; sing, all you who are upright in heart!

In Psalm 33, he says to "sing joyfully, praise the Lord by making music and sing to Him a new song."

In Psalm 34:8-9, he invites us to "Taste and see that the Lord is good; blessed is the one who takes refuge in him. Fear the Lord, you his holy people, for those who fear him lack nothing."

You have to remember that this is coming from the guy who killed the bear and the giant. Because of his life experience, you can trust him when he says, "those who fear Him lack nothing." Remember to use your story for God's glory.

In Psalm 37, he tells us, "Do not fret. Trust in the Lord. Take delight in the Lord. Commit your way. Be still and wait patiently. Refrain from anger."

Wow. It sure sounds like a lot of coaching and encouragement to me. He commands us to act in faith. Psalm 55:22 says, "Cast your cares on the Lord and he will sustain you; he will never let the righteous be shaken."

In Psalm 66:3, David says, "Say to God, 'How awesome are

your deeds! Your enemies cringe before your mighty power.'" (NLT)

Psalm 105:4-5 tells us to "Look to the Lord and his strength; seek his face always. Remember the wonders he has done." (Emphasis all mine)

His words are entirely action-driven. Yet, I don't think I've ever heard anyone describe David as bossy. I've never heard anyone say that David was *making* generations of Jesus followers worship. So why have we said that, or allowed that to be said, of our modern worship leaders on Sunday morning? It seems that there is a certain amount of instruction, challenge, invitation, and example needed to LEAD WORSHIP. We easily forget, which is why we need the reminder to remember His goodness and to sing out in praise to the Lord, in response!

Just as faith without works is dead, I believe leading worship without instruction and invitation is dead. Leading others will require you to not only model worship, but talk them through *how* to worship.

Worship leading according to scripture and David's example includes much instruction. There is a call and a command to declare the praises of the King no matter what the circumstances may look like. What are you inviting those who you lead to do? Think about it and define it clearly with action words. Our job is to fan the flame for the one whose spark is dying out. Our task is to hold up the arms of the one who is so tired of the battle and ready to give up. We are to prayerfully plan and listen to the heart of the Father as we practice and prepare, shining the light and pointing the way so that worshippers will see and know He is God. May we turn on the music and make way for the praise of the Lord God Almighty to be on their lips.

Make Me Believe You: Worshiping in Action, Posture, and Expression

Chapter Seven

I am so thankful that God gave us a picture within the scriptures of how to effectively lead worship. God's Word is a treasure that we can continue to discover new revelation from each time we study it. When I examined David's life a little more in depth, the third thing I noticed is that **he expressed his worship with action.**

Psalm 95:6-7 says, "Come, let us worship and bow down. Let us kneel before the Lord our maker, for he is our God. We are the people he watches over, the flock under his care." (NLT)

There are actually three different Hebrew words used in that passage for both our worship and the reverence of bowing down in reverence with humility.

- Shachah: To bow down, before God in worship.
- Kara: To bend, kneel, bow, bow down, sink down to one's knees.
- Barak: To kneel and bless God.

I'm pretty sure that a point was being made. The action was

being emphasized here to ensure that we would get the message. Repetition does that for the hearer.

David bowed before the Lord in humility, in reverence, and out of respect. From watching fairy tales, and even in this current age, we've seen someone curtsy or bow down in the presence of a king or queen. It is a way to bestow honor upon someone. David modeled this in his worship to the Eternal God. Even as a king, he humbled himself to worship the only One who is King of kings.

After David became King of Israel, he conquered the Philistines with an army of 30,000. He then made plans to bring back the Ark of God to the city of David. After this victory, scripture tells us that David and the people of Israel were celebrating, singing songs and making music before the Lord. 2 Samuel 6:14 says, "David was dancing before the Lord with all his might." In celebration of victory, it's completely alright if you feel the need to move a little bit. Depending on your denomination, you may be more at peace with this than others. But, if David can dance before the Lord, then we can certainly tap our feet, clap our hands, wave our arms back and forth, and even jump up and down. Our God is good and He extends freedom and victory to us in every area of our lives. That is worth celebrating with every fiber of our beings! Dancing and movement is Biblical. I will share more in-depth about using motions effectively in chapters 15 and 16.

Psalm 63:3-4 says, "Because your love is better than life, my lips will glorify you. I will praise you as long as I live, and in your name I will lift up my hands." The word praise in verse 4 is *Shabach* in Hebrew, and it means "to praise, commend, boast in a loud voice." But something else we see in this verse is how David models lifting up His hands in worship.

Lifting our hands in worship is a way of showing surrender.

When I lift my hands I am showing honor to God, but I'm also saying, I'm all in God. You can have all of me. I give you all of me. I will not hold anything back in order to honor You.

I also share about lifting our hands because it's an important reminder that it's a way of saying, "God I need you." It places us in a posture of complete and total dependence on our Father.

Action, Posture, and Expression

I like to ask a group of kids if they have a younger sibling at home. And if so, have they ever noticed their little brother or sister walking up to one of their parents, standing in front of them, and lifting their hands up. What does this mean when they do that? They start shouting, "they want to be picked up!" Exactly. When you lift your hands to the Lord you're also saying, "God, I need Your help. Hold me. Pick me up in Your arms. I need to feel safe." Worship is a hiding place in God's presence. When we draw near to God, He draws near to us. If we reach out to Him with our hands lifted high, we will see and know God on a deeper, more intimate level.

I truly believe that our posture matters in worship. One of my favorite pieces I've ever read about this subject is by Stephen Miller. It's entitled, *"Why Posture Matters In Worship."* I beg you to google it and read the article on The Gospel Coalition's website.

Here is a short excerpt:

> *When a young man meets a young woman that he wants to impress, he stands up straight, shoulders back, gut sucked in. He maintains eye contact and a smile. When he wants to propose, he gets down on one knee. When he has messed up royally and*

needs to apologize, it's two knees. If someone points a gun at you, your hands rise in surrender. If your children want you to hold them or lavish affection on them, they raise their arms. At sporting events, when your team scores, you jump in the air, pump your fists, and shout as loudly as you can. When the ref makes a bad call, you throw your hands up in frustration and boo vigorously. Your heart is caught up in the experience of the moment, which causes your body to respond outwardly. We were created as holistic beings with intellects, emotions, and bodies all working in concert with one another to express ourselves. Depending on the study, we learn that anywhere from 70 percent to 95 percent of communication is non-verbal. We say a lot about what we think and feel without uttering a single word.

Our body naturally acts the way our hearts feel. So we see encouragements throughout Scripture to bow humbly, raise hands joyfully, shout and sing loudly, clap hands, and even dance before the Lord.

King David, the innovator of music in corporate worship, wrote hundreds of songs for the purpose of engaging the mind, heart, and body in worship. He understood that posture outwardly expresses an inward reality.

Sweet Sound

The fruit of our outward expressiveness reveals the root of our hearts.

I believe that last statement is so powerful. It's powerful because it's true. **The fruit of our outward expressiveness reveals the root of our hearts.** Selah.

It's true in every other area of our lives, as well. A romantic relationship. Our favorite team's sporting event. Our own child's sporting event. Your new favorite song on the radio. The countenance on your face when you're watching your favorite show. Even the most stoic of faces express emotion. God gave us those eyebrows for a reason. Raise them. Turn that frown upside down!

Still, we encounter Christians who will use plenty of excuses. I have friends who have expressed why they don't perceive their expression of worship matters. For the person who you're thinking of in your church that says, "I love Jesus. I just don't like worship," the issue is there is some other area in his or her life I guarantee you they will react with expression. It may look like a shout. It could be a smile that stretches from ear to ear. It could be laughter, a spin around the room, or a squeal. You name it. If you can react with a happy dance in your kitchen when you get a check in the mail for your birthday or a refund on your tax return, then you can absolutely react with expression to the Maker of Heaven and earth. It may be jubilee. It may be tears. It could be a victory dance. For others, a fist pump. It may look like kneeling down. It could be outstretched arms. It's singing. It's shouting. It's praying. It's being still. It's moving and marching. It's art. It's writing. It's a beautiful dance. It's someone very skilled at his or her craft who is honoring God with it. It's a combination of all of those things, because we are living beings created by a living God.

When we comprehend how big the galaxies are, yet He knows our names, catches our tears in a bottle, numbers our days, and even the hairs on our heads, how can we not respond in worship with our whole being? Not just in our thoughts or our words, but with our faces and our bodies. Reverence. Honor. Surrender. Let *everything* within me bless His holy name!

Psalm 103:1 says, "With my whole heart, with my whole life, and with my innermost being, I bow in wonder and love before you, the holy God!" (TPT) I think Bob Goff said it best when he described it as "God wanting your whole room. Not just a drawer in your dresser or a spot cleared off of the night stand." Too often we give Him a piece of who we are. We let Him have a spot in our lives. That's simply not enough. He wants it all. He deserves it all. Let's take action. Take things out and clean up. Encourage those you lead to make space and give Him their ALL.

Our Battle
Plan

Chapter Eight

The fourth example we learn from David's life is **how to fight our battles through worship**, which may be the most important one yet.

Life will never be void of battles. You and I both know that. Life will dish out trouble from time to time, but it's how we respond to hardship that makes all the difference. David wasn't perfect, but he put in the work by pursuing the Lord over and over again. It was his reflex to run to the Father. As he consistently pursued God through his praise, God certainly turned His face upon him and granted him favor and blessing in unparalleled ways. As both a worshipper and worship leader, David carried the war cry of praise, which led to the victories he experienced. 2 Samuel 8:6 says, "The Lord gave David victory wherever he went." That's what I want it to be said of me. You can even put it on my tombstone: *The Lord gave Yancy victory wherever she went.*

Spiritual warfare is first and foremost fought through our worship. A few years ago, I attended a women's event where I heard Christian recording artist, Ginny Owens, share about the Psalms. She said, "They preach the truth that they know to their souls. Keep speaking what your mind knows until your heart catches up." This is what we see consistently throughout the Psalms. They put the faithfulness and goodness of God on repeat. Because you know what? If we keep speaking it and singing it, we will begin to believe it. Our spirits will rise up with boldness as we express our faith. Our confidence is built in the character of who God is because of the repeated habit of giving God praise.

It's safe to say that we've all heard the scripture from Luke 6:45 that says, "Out of the abundance of the heart the mouth speaks." (NRSV) Think of your words as the trajectory of an elevator. You can think it in your mind, but God's Word tells us to take every thought captive (2 Cor. 10:5). The only way for the things to get from your mind to your heart is by stopping at your mouth. What you speak will get into your heart. Lead your kids in songs that will remind hearts what is true about God. This is how you prepare them for the battles of life. If you want them to fight their battles in worship as an adult, then you need to let them learn how to as they navigate childhood.

In my own life, I've gone through intense seasons of loss and brokenness. I remember when my world as I knew it came crashing down. It was literally like a house of cards where you see the pieces floating mid-air in slow motion. It hurt. I was in pain. I was sad. I felt like the rug had been pulled out from under me. I knew that I didn't have the strength, mastermind, or right connections to magically make it all better. The house needed to be rebuilt, but I had no idea how. It was in this season where my faith was thoroughly tested. It was in this place that I knew confidently that I could not fix it. My only hope was to place the pieces in God's hands and allow Him to make a beautiful story for His glory. In the years that followed, I was able to connect with a couple old friends who had their own messy stories of life disasters and hurt from the Church. On both occasions after our time together, I received similar messages from these friends. One commented, "I'm so impressed that you didn't lose your faith through all of this." She was speaking from her own experience and hurt. My heart still breaks thinking about that conversation. But her comment helped me see the differences in where we had placed our trust. I responded, "I knew I couldn't fix it. It was beyond my control or power. My only choice was to allow God to take the broken pieces and allow Him to heal and help me." I have learned that God is always good, even when His people aren't. Never confuse the two. If Christians hurt you and that affects your faith in God, then you've put your faith in people, not in the Lord. In my brokenness, I worshiped. I wrote songs with faith-filled words to speak and declare not what my reality was, but what I knew God's power was capable of. Through these conversations, I realized how important it is for us to teach kids how to run to God in everything they face.

When they are disappointed, to find hope in the Lord.

When they are hurting, to allow God to bring peace.

When they are sick, to have faith that Jesus is their healer.

When they are sad, to find their strength in the joy that He gives.

When they are lost, to find their purpose in who He created them to be.

When they feel broken, to cast their cares at His feet, trusting God will restore and make them whole.

I want the kids we are leading to know the path to run to God, no matter what. That we'll be just like David, whose automatic reflex was to worship. I believe worship is the exercise that we do in order to develop that muscle. Rather than turning to the things of this world to numb the pain, what if we raised a generation of boys and girls that drew closer to the Father when life starts to beat them up? Instead of retreating, what if they took steps to approach His throne? What if His very presence was the armor that they needed to make it through this thing we call life? I can't imagine navigating my life without Him.

I can't imagine surviving and moving forward from the pain I've encountered without Him. I don't want to lead kids to run to social media when they are hurting. I don't want to encourage them to turn to food or drinks to get through. I want to teach them how to approach God's throne with awe and wonder. How do you do that? By helping them practice. By teaching and showing them by example. Choose now to show kids how to fight their battles in praise. Don't push it off and expect them to figure it out as college students. If you want them to worship when they are 50, or even in their thirties, then you must begin the process when they are five and develop it when they are in the fifth grade. You learn by practicing. Give space for them to learn at an early age.

I'd love to share a Facebook post that I wrote one day to encourage children's ministers. It's a journal entry of sorts, and I pray it will encourage you, as well:

> *For those who don't know my story, I'm a PK. My Dad is Jim Wideman and has done Kidmin since the late 70s. Because of my lifelong experience around children's ministry and my Dad's faithfulness to impact kids, I've had a front row seat to witness what happens long term when you welcome children and show them Jesus. No doubt today was full of hard work. You may have put out fires and very well could be working through some hard challenges with volunteers, staff, and leadership above you. Because of the history I have witnessed, I have a glimpse into your future —that you can't even imagine from where you are now. Allow me to*

pull back the curtain to show you what happens.

These children you are loving, teaching, and blessing don't stay kids forever. They grow up. They become adults who go on to be Miss America, pastors, missionaries, rockstars, doctors, and faithful church-going Christians who raise their own families. What you did today wasn't about today. It was about their future. The imprint you make lasts a lifetime. The seeds you plant take root and grow. Those seeds also plant more seeds and the harvest grows even greater.

As I scrolled through Instagram today, I saw one of those "kids" my Dad ministered to. His own son is now 18 and preaching a sermon to the adult congregation of his church. Then, my family had a visit from one of the "once upon a time kids" who is now 47 and has children in college. She wasn't someone who had a perfect childhood or family life...but God. As I glanced over and saw both her hands raised to Heaven in worship, my heart knew that someone needed me to share what happens when you fast forward 40 years. What you are doing has eternal purpose. You are making a difference because fruit is born from the work you do.

The ripple effect of our obedience goes far beyond

what we can see and the people we know. Don't stop doing what God has called you to do. The harvest is ripe.

What you do isn't about Sunday. It's about their future.

I love you and I'm cheering you on.

They don't stay kids forever. They grow up, get married, have families, and live abundant and, even complicated, lives. While they are still young children, I teach them to participate in worship because I want them to worship even when they're going through a midlife crisis. And still be worshiping when a family member receives a cancer diagnosis. May they continue as they navigate a job change and choose to remain faithful to a spouse. I want to be able to say that I taught them how to run to the Father in everything they will face. Worship is the doorway to His presence. It's how we enter His gates. I once heard a song that describes our praise as a highway to God's heart. There are no instant quick-fixes in God's Kingdom. His time is not ours, but I can personally attest that if you're believing for something in your life, your praise elevates you to VIP status. There are benefits to seeking after God's heart through worship.

David was passionately after God's heart. It defined who He was and how He lived for the Lord. There are many titles we could seek to attain. There are positions of stature and awards we can desire, but in the end, those things are fleeting and will pass away. You will never regret taking part in a worship service. You will never wish you had given God less of your attention. Psalm 100:3 says, "Know that the Lord is God. It is he who made us, and we are his; we are his people, the sheep of his pasture." David understood the role of the shepherd and the role of the sheep. I believe he gave us a gift within his writing so that we can better understand what being part of the flock of God truly means.

I often screenshot quotes I find that I want to keep and remember for future reference. I want to share a few of the things that I've kept over the years that some awesome worship leaders, pastors, and teachers have shared about worship. Use these to learn. Use these to teach your kids about worship.

- *"You can live in worry or live in worship, but you can't do both."* - Jon Purkey
- *"The password to your miracle is the sound of your praise."* - John Gray
- *"Worship overwhelms the thing that's overwhelming you."* - @Crosspoint_TV
- *"Worship stops the noise of life."* – Darlene Zschech
- *In the movie "Sing" they said, "Your song is your weapon." What weapon are you sending forth by the song you sing?*
- *"Worship is a weapon that pierces the darkness and leads us into light."* – Louie Giglio
- *"Worship is a declaration of war against everything that says God can't."* – Louie Giglio
- *"Praise will lift your perspective to see God's promise in your problem."* - Steve Furtick
- *"Worship isn't merely a "yes" to the God who saves, but also a resounding and furious "NO"*

to the lies that echo in the mountains around us."
– Mike Cosper, from Rhythms of Grace
- *"When you praise through your darkest hours, you turn your prison into a pulpit." – Alex Seeley*

I attended a private Christian school for a few years before my family began homeschooling. I can still picture the classroom. I've never forgotten that they had us memorize Psalm 100 when I was in the second grade. It's a short Psalm, but it really covers the basics of how to worship and why we partake in it. Take these scriptures to heart. Use them to form a vision for how you want to lead kids to be after God's heart just as David was.

Shout for joy to the Lord, all the earth.
Worship the Lord with gladness;
come before him with joyful songs.
Know that the Lord is God.
It is he who made us, and we are his;
we are his people, the sheep of his pasture.
Enter his gates with thanksgiving
and his courts with praise;
give thanks to him and praise his name.
For the Lord is good and his love endures forever;
his faithfulness continues through all generations

David's battle plan was to worship. The Lord gave him victory wherever he went.

I want that for my family.

I want that for the kids and families I have the privilege to lead.

I want that for you and your family.

I want that for the kids and families you have the privilege to lead.

We must equip those who we lead to fight the spiritual battles that they will encounter. The way of the Lord is not of this world. In typical fashion of our God, we fight our battles not with swords or weapons, but with the Word of our testimony and the sound of our praise.

Evaluation is a
Strength

Although I'm pretty sure I could have spent the entire book talking about David and why he was such a great worship leader, (yes, I love him that much) I'm only going to share one more nugget of wisdom from David's example. Before we wrap up this section, I want to remind you to open your Bible and see what you can learn from David. Ask God to speak to you and reveal insights and revelation as to how you need to move forward in leading worship like David. I trust that God will speak to you now and in the years to come. Invite Him into the process.

The fifth and final takeaway from the life of David is that he **modeled evaluation and showed us that change is necessary.**

David was aware that exclusively relying on praises he had sung in prior years wasn't going to cut it. We don't see where David cried out, "Remember five years ago when I worshiped You at youth camp with that song from the radio?" He doesn't ask, "Do you remember when I sang one of the songs of old from the hymnal?" We don't arrive at a level of worship completion. It's continuous for all eternity. Old songs are good. Current songs are good. But scripture specifically highlights the command to sing new songs. Psalm 149:1 says, "Sing to the Lord a new song, his praise in the assembly of his faithful people." That is a piece of instruction. It's a command. He's telling us what to sing. Have you ever had a goosebump moment in worship when they introduced a new song? Maybe the song had a message that connected with the season you're in, giving you words you needed to sing, declare, and prophesy into your future. That new song could have highlighted a character quality of God that you had not thought about before. I believe new songs are important. I go into a great deal about introducing new songs in chapter 14.

We serve a living God. Although He doesn't change, He and His Word are active and living. Those who you lead are living and growing, too. They have seasons of life just like the seasons we encounter and the fruit that harvests in due time. Even if you've been at the same church working with the same age group for the past 20 years, I'm sure you have noticed that kids' interests, likes, and favorite things have changed in those two decades. Just as music and fashion styles cycle through and shift, humans experience many changes in their lives.

One of my favorite things that my Dad has said in the past few years is his awareness that "the difference between fresh fruit and canned fruit is that the latter is fruit from another season." He was sharing this about the work and ministry he does. He didn't want to only rely on past successes and victories. There are plenty who still minister from the bounty of "canned fruit." Dad was sharing that it's his desire to be faithful and obedient now as he tills the fields and puts his hand to the plow in his church and ministry, so he would grow and reap fresh fruit for this season. Wow! There is so much truth that we, as leaders, ministers, and individuals, can learn from that. Just let that one marinate and simmer in order to challenge you.

What songs do you need to STOP doing? Are you still forcing songs a couple times a month that were once the bomb dot com in your ministry, but lately have been limping along, lacking ability to connect to your kids? Let them go. Release them into history.

One of the best hours of my leadership life was spent talking with one of our preteen students. I had been wrestling with a couple new songs that I was on the fence about introducing. Sometimes those decisions are crystal clear and you know it's a must add. Other times it seems like a good idea, but that guarantee factor isn't there. That's where you bring in other members of your team and in this case, students, to play the song and see how it strikes them. I'd rather do my research off stage so I can work hard to see that what I present on stage will indeed connect and be a win. So, I started off asking Madison about each new song I was considering. She was a staff kid and was hanging out in her mom's office, because, if memory serves me correct, schools had closed that day due to weather. I invited her to my office and solicited her opinion. The feedback and reactions I received about each of these new songs was indeed beneficial, so I had the idea to ask her about the songs we were currently doing in our preteen ministry.

I pulled out my binder of weekly worship sets and began naming songs. (Yes, for many reasons, you need to keep a list of what you're singing each week so you'll have it for reference in times of planning and evaluation.) Singing a portion, or even playing a bit of it when needed, in order to trigger her memory, was worth the insight I gained. Let's be real, though. At times, she tried not to hurt my feelings and gave me a half-hearted response about a song, but I quickly figured it out as we went. But, when I saw the big, exuberant, excited reaction about other songs, I took notes accordingly. (Insert smirk.) This girl was a pretty popular kid, so she wasn't just telling me what *she* thought, but also what other kids had said. There were times she shared, "the girls like this one but the boys don't." Well, well, well. I could use that information. It doesn't mean I pull the plug and never do the song again because the boys didn't like it. But, it does help in being more strategic with how often I choose that song or where I place it in a set. She gave other feedback like, "Oh, we're kind of getting tired of that one." That was amazing to hear because the songs still worked in class when we did them. But, how helpful to get that feedback and slam the brakes on how often I use a song. Then, it can serve us for a longer stretch of time by spreading out its use a bit, instead of overusing and breaking it.

I totally get that if you're working with preschoolers, then gaining this kind of feedback could be tricky. But if you're working with elementary kids, it's doable. Maybe you have a group of kids on a leadership team who you could pull aside and ask these questions, as well. Maybe you recruit a handful of kids to attend a special "Music Feedback Team" panel a few times a year. Serve them ice cream or pizza and just pick their brain for an hour. I guarantee you'll leave the time with valuable insight that will help you determine which songs need to be shelved for a time, and what the common denominators are about their absolute favorite songs. Use all of that info and data to help you choose songs in the future.

I would also challenge you to get the perspective of other leaders. There have been times that my perspective on stage caused me to think something had bombed, only to walk off stage and have other leaders tell me how sweet God's presence was in the room that day. Or, they will share something about a child who was sitting close to them that I didn't see or notice. Alternatively, there have been days that I thought everything went great. I thought it had been one of the best ever, only to talk with other members of the team and have them share a different perspective. Your view from the stage isn't the same as the leaders in the back of the room, standing on the side and amongst the kids. Don't expect that you have it all figured out. Talk to them. Ask questions. Solicit feedback. Take the meat. Cut out and dispose of the fat. Use the knowledge to refine what you do.

Plan and allow for time to be creative. Daily, weekly, and monthly. Years ago, I read an amazing book by Twyla Tharp called *"The Creative Habit."* I learned that in order to be creative you have to know how to prepare to be creative. There's a process that generates creativity, and you can learn it and make it habitual. Remember that you are a creative being because you were made in the image of a creative God.

I believe constructive feedback and evaluation of results is a necessary step to growth. Think about your ministry and answer these questions:

- How do you teach kids each week why we worship? (whether it's the reasons we sing, clap, lift our hands, show honor to God, etc.)
- How do you have people model ways to participate?
- How do you encourage the boys in your class to get involved?
- How have you seen growth over the past six months in the ways your kids worship?

These things are moving targets for you. The current path could be totally different than the place you will need to lead from six or twelve months from now. The important thing is that you are seeing growth. You're seeing steps taken and ground gained. Your next steps should contain a different list than the steps for this same time a year from now, and so forth.

I can't stress how important it is to reflect back from time to time. Set a periodic reminder in your calendar to think through the wins and the progress that was made. When we're in forward motion, it's easy to be hyper aware that we haven't reached the place we want to be at yet. Maybe you've even been discouraged on the journey because you haven't arrived where you wanted your kids to be. It's okay. Sometimes you're so focused on the destination that you don't take the time to acknowledge the growth and progress that's been made. What are the steps that they've taken? What are the wins that you've seen? Who is the kid that you thought would be the last one to start singing, but started participating eight weeks ago? See, I told you there's been progress. Reflect on how you have seen God moving. Maybe it was the kid who knelt down in worship or prayed a prayer full of faith. Set aside time to periodically make a list of the victories you have experienced. It will be beneficial in the moments when you hear that voice saying, *"You're not getting anywhere. Is it really worth it?"* Remind yourself of the growth you have seen. Keep your vision ahead of you. Practically imagine creative ways you can lead songs and teach your kids, so they can learn by doing and experiencing week by week. I promise that not one of you will stay in the same place. You *will* grow.

I understand how it is in ministry when there's a big shift in vision and you're excited because of where you're headed, but it feels like you're wading through waist-deep oceans of molasses. You can get irritated. You become frustrated and start to question if any of it's worth it because you're not where you want to be…yet.

Maybe you're currently in the middle of that season. You could have recently made changes in who leads your worship time. You could be trying to inject new songs into your standard set. You could even be confident that the changes you've made are in fact good and right. But, you're not seeing the kind of progress that you had hoped you would.

May I invite you to not become weary in well-doing? (Galatians 6:9) Do not give up. I repeat: *Do not give up.*

Think of this process of change and steering the ship in a new direction toward the heavenly shore, as a garden. I'm sure we would all love to have the perfect yard and flower beds, and maybe even win our neighborhood's "Yard of the Month" award (if your neighborhood has one of those). But, something I've noticed about people who have meticulous grass, flowers, and plants is that it takes a lot of work. Any transformation process of remodeling and improving requires time, dedication, and work. You have to be willing to get your hands dirty and go in and rip out the things that aren't supposed to be there. It's not enough to simply buy weed killer at the home improvement store and then spray it. You have to rip things out at their root system and remove them. It could mean you'll need to feed the ground with fertilizer and nutrients to encourage life. You'll likely plant a few new things that you want to take root. You will have to water, wait, and then, repeat. Along the way, you'll have to remove the weeds, roots and all. At times, you'll have to prune and trim the plants as they grow. It's not just a decide you want it, plant some new stuff, and voila "yard of the month award" process. It will take time, nurturing, planting, watering, weeding, trimming, and repeating it all, year after year. But, the good news is you will yield the results you desire when you do not give up. Do not give up, my friend. Continue to show up and be faithful to the process. It will yield fruit, in due time.

Rhythms of
Worship for
Each Generation

Chapter Ten

Have you ever stopped to think about what kind of worshiper you want the adults in your congregation to be?

I believe an active mission of every church should be to help believers step into their God-given identities. Worshiping God is one of our greatest purposes, and who we were designed to be. Although many churches check the worship box off the list each week, I feel there is still much to be desired in how we are leading others to encounter the presence of Jesus during our corporate times of worship. I have a burden to teach this generation so they'll better understand why we worship God and what that looks like in their daily lives. No matter what seat you have at the table, I believe you can shine a light on this need and help trailblaze a path that could transform how your church leads and participates in worship for decades to come. This is generational. It will be impactful not only for the current season, but for the future life of your church.

Will this be easy? Probably not. Will it be comfortable? Not always. Will it feel like work at times? You betcha. Will It be worth it? Absolutely. 100%.

One thing I've noticed when ministries work as silos, as opposed to having a strategy and mission behind the method, is that worship happens all over the map. I'm sure you have seen it before, or maybe you're even living it right now. I promise, I'm not spying on you. I've really seen this far too many times to count. You have one age level that has great worship where people are engaged and then another age group that has weak leadership and, let's be real, a major disconnect. In some churches, kids worship is the strongest, whereas the student and adult worship ministry is weak. Other churches have strong student ministry worship, while kids worship is clueless and adult worship is one step away from being a museum. You could have a church with fantastic adult worship, but kids and/or students are a total afterthought. Far too often we have seen worship happening at various speeds and levels of intentionality within the four walls of our churches because there's no overall vision for worship.

Let's say you were planning to open a restaurant. You sought out fantastic chefs to build your menu. Each person had been hired for a specific reason based on skill set, talent, and experience. There was something unique that they could contribute to what you were creating. So, in an effort of delegation, you divided up the task of creating your menu. You gave one person the role of *Small Plates/Appetizers*. Another had the responsibility of *Entrees and Main Courses*. Then, you hired a different chef to craft the *Side Dishes and Dessert* menu. Fast forward a few weeks later to the first menu tasting. People worked tirelessly. The anticipation in the room was palpable. They had been diligent at using the creativity and skills they had mastered to create something delicious. They prepared these sample plates for you to taste. The starters look exciting. They may even taste magnificent! You begin to envision the Yelp reviews of the local food critics as you chew and savor the flavors. As you move on to taste test the entrees, you become very aware that you have a problem on your hands. When

Sweet Sound

When one builds a building, whether it's a home or for commercial use, it's common sense that you don't begin with the roof or the locks on the doors, even though both of those are a must to provide long-term safety. My husband and I built our home a dozen or so years ago. I distinctly remember that there's a specific order the process must go in to take an empty lot and turn it into a home for a family to dwell. There's a lot of digging that takes place initially. The Lord knows we are thankful for the modern advancement of plumbing and what that means for our kitchen and restrooms. Let's give Him thanks right now. Glory!

Once they've dug and prepared the site, they pour footers because they have a plan for what's going to happen. Next comes the foundation, mixed with a little bit of waiting as things settle and dry. But oh how glorious is the strength and solidarity of that foundation! Then, they plug into the larger plumbing systems within the neighborhood and city. I remember how exciting it was when progression was made for the lumber to be put together to frame our home. There was so much you could finally envision when you saw those walls, albeit see-through, going up. The frame was followed by wiring and insulation. Those would be difference makers in the seasons of life when the temperatures rise and the weary winters begin to freeze. Every stage and phase of the project is crucial. There's a timeline that must be followed in order to build something that will last for years to come. I'm sure we've all heard stories of a construction project that tried to cut some corners and ended up having detrimental results that cost more work and money in the end than if they had yielded to the methods, inspections, and processes set in place from the beginning.

Once the foundation is set and the walls, wiring, and insulation go in, it's exciting to see the place no longer as a construction zone, but it visibly become an actual home. You start to see it all coming together. You begin to imagine evenings hanging out with family and friends while celebrating holidays, milestones, and Friday nights. Sheetrock, paint, trim work, finishes, décor. Layer by layer, each one is one step closer to making it an environment for family to be home.

I want to invite you to think about the path your church takes for worship just like the path of a construction project.

Plans and Digging = The hard work of asking questions of your staff and leadership. Seeking God for what He wants for your house of worship. When you close your eyes and dream of what could be, what do you see?

Pouring the footers = Write the vision and make it plain. What is God telling you? When you look at the plans, what does the vision dictate? What are the next steps you are determining you need to take in order to end up where you're wanting to go? What do you long to see happen in the months and years ahead? Take a look at the plans. Then measure, design, and organize for those things to come into fruition. Build a structure that can support the pipeline you're connecting from room to room and ministry area to other ministry area.

Foundation = Making it happen. One week at a time. One service at a time. Build the foundation layer by layer. Word by word. Song by song. Psalm by Psalm. Give people knowledge and understanding to help them know, grow, and understand what worship is.

Frame, wiring and insulation = Once the foundation is poured, the project isn't over. You build upon it. You let them try worship on for themselves and start practicing by doing it. Worship is a hiding place in His presence. Wire them with the understanding that it is more than just a preliminary part of a service before the preacher speaks. Teach your people how to run to God in whatever they face. They will need that insulation throughout the years to keep them safe, warm, and able to continue fighting the good fight of faith regardless of what crazy weather pattern blows their way.

Sheetrock, paint, finishes and décor = There are phases to a project and to life. As the process moves along, what you need to teach and how you lead your people forward could shift and change. Kind of like the popularity of gold then silver, to black then bronze, and back to gold bathroom hardware. Oh boy. You will likely even see staff members change from time to time. Kids will graduate. Families will move to another state. Change is inevitable.

You may go through these processes and determine five years from now that you need to revisit these conversations. Maybe you underestimated what you could dream. The process may have been harder or moved slower than what you imagined. You can always adjust. The idea is that this is a living and moving thing happening in the life of our church body. The goal is to raise up disciples who love to worship. Let's help kids, students, and adults understand that Father God loves to hear their voices sing His praises. Just as a parent loves to receive a heartfelt expression from their child, we are children of God and oh how He longs to be near us and have our hearts tethered to His. Worship is the foundation upon which we build our lives as followers of Christ.

Whether it be when he is speaking, teaching leaders at a conference, through his leadership club, or coaching pastors, I can hear my Dad saying, "Start with the end in mind."

So, may I challenge you to do that? **Start with the end in mind.** Ask this question: What kind of worshipers do you want adults in your congregation to be? Once you answer that, you can begin to work in reverse as you determine what the various stages of discipleship in this area may look like for your congregation. As you start with the end in mind, you then begin to work backward to define and develop what the goal needs to be for each age group and classroom within your church. You have 936 Sundays in the life of a young person. That's over 900 opportunities, as you gather, to help kids fall in love with Jesus through intentional times of worship and discipleship.

Help toddlers and preschoolers WORSHIP.

Help elementary kids WORSHIP.

Help preteens WORSHIP.

Help middle schoolers WORSHIP.

Help high schoolers WORSHIP.

Help college students and young adults WORSHIP.

Help adults of every age and season WORSHIP.

Help senior citizens WORSHIP.

You can accomplish seeing that vision come to pass by starting the process from the very beginning. Start in the nursery by playing intentional playlists, or having a time your caregivers sing over *and with* these babies as they gurgle the choruses of praise that belong to God. In the preschool ministry of your church, give them the right bite-size pieces for this phase of life. Choose songs they can easily understand. Vocabulary, repetition, and activity are some key ingredients. Then, continue to build upon that foundation in the elementary ministry. Help their understanding and expression of worship grow and develop. It doesn't end there. The roots can grow deeper as a preteen, and even as a middle schooler. Wire them to worship as a reflex. Host worship nights so they can practice. Share songs and playlists throughout the week to invite them to shift their focus from the sounds and voices of this world to the song of Heaven. The impact spans even greater as a high school student. Think of it like a set of steps. One step leads to the next and then the next. Just as you don't leap up a set of steps (unless you're a total daredevil type), you will gradually lead them up one step at a time. One phase of life at a time. Level upon level. But through the months and years ahead, oh my goodness, get ready. You'll be able to look at how far they've traveled and who their spirit man became over the process.

My pastor, Alex Seeley, has said this about how Sunday church should be: "I believe the church should be a place that causes you to have a thirst and hunger for more of the Word and more of His presence so that you go seek it out as well. We don't spoon feed "there's your hour and a half for the week. Goodbye." It's a taste and see that the Lord is good and it leaves you wanting more. The Holy Spirit always satisfies but leaves you wanting more."

You can completely change the way that worship is cultivated within the life of your congregation, over the span of one generation. The possibility of results from this effort is to have men and women who understand that worship is a communication tool they possess in order to respond to God and engage in conversation with Him. What a win! I want to cultivate a rhythm in the hearts of God's people who long to be in the safety of His presence.

Psalm 145:3-4 says, "Great is the Lord! He is most worthy of praise! No one can measure his greatness. Let each generation tell its children of your mighty acts; let them proclaim your power." (NLT) This should be the vision of every church. To see each generation proclaiming the goodness of God through praise.

These processes could also lead to building a team that can serve in multiple areas. There could be positions and rooms where you develop musicians and worship leaders to serve your church for years to come. Think of a farm club style system, like in the sports world. In the church where I worked, I was blessed that the vision for worship was united. We had people who served and led worship in multiple age groups. We had musicians that played in more than one class. People and roles could interchange seamlessly. We had areas where someone might begin to serve for the first time. This could have to do with their skill set or level of ability. Your gift makes room for you. As experience is gained and faithfulness is proved, you may see fit to provide opportunities and open doors for members of the team to serve and lead others.

It was a joy to mentor individuals and watch them grow as we set bars for them that they eventually grew past. Coaching leaders and seeing them have a moment on stage where the things finally clicked that we had previously talked through was so rewarding. They led with authority and spirit-led leadership, and you could sense the difference in a tangible way. The light bulb went off for them. I remember the joy of watching faithful young people eventually serve on our adult worship teams. I would go watch them on the "big stage" like a proud mom does, tissue in hand.

Every room and every stage is important.

Every group isn't just an audience, but children of the Most High God who we have the privilege of helping turn their gaze and affection on Jesus.

Worship happening in another room isn't competition to what you do in your ministry area's time of worship. For every age, worshiping God is a key part of why we assemble together, as well as in our personal walk with Christ. As you begin this conversation and develop a relationship with other leaders in your church, **I believe what you can accomplish together will be far greater than what**

you could ever do on your own.

You may decide to change the structure of worship and who ultimately heads that up churchwide. Or, you may find a common vision that each ministry area continues to lead, with check-ins and check-ups along the way to help each member stay on task and be united in the process. I believe in your ability to seek the Lord and ask Him for fresh vision and wisdom for the house you are building and caring for. I know He will speak to you as you develop the foundation and construct teams and individuals who will be hungry for more of His presence, and will ultimately lead the way for others to get there as well. I know that even in the times of pruning and repotting He will guide you as you work and put in the hard labor it takes to see any garden flourish.

I can't wait to see the harvest that comes from the seeds you plant. I heard it said once that "whatever you give yourself to will grow." It was one of those statements that I pondered and chewed on for a while. It's wisdom for many areas of our lives. I believe it is wisdom for you today as you pray about those under your care. As you think through the progression of steps and phases of life that a member of your church family goes through, ask yourself: *How can I better help them grow in their knowledge and expression of worship?* I dream of a Church that focuses on the believer's heart for worship. Cultivating a rhythm in our hearts for the generations that we shepherd and lead. What you give yourself to will indeed grow.

We are better together.

There's no harmony in a solo.

It's time to step up and take the lead. This conversation has merit. It's a worthy task to explore and trailblaze a path for the generations that will follow.

Rhythms of Worship for Each Generation

From birth until death, conduct a symphony of praise that will echo from one generation to the next. Like a wave rolls in and out, growing bigger in the ocean. Just as the reverb sound expands, repeats, and sustains. There is so much more than most of us have tasted. Let's unite our vision, our hearts, and the worship we sing until every knee bows and every tongue confesses Jesus is Lord!

Developing the
Palates of Children

Chapter Eleven

I have led worship for every age. Birth until death is how I like to put it. There are nuances about leading every age group, but I am fully convinced children are the easiest group to lead in worship. It's naturally in us to worship. It's naturally in us to be drawn to the things of God, and to the heart of our Father. Kids are closest to the beginning point. They've allowed less junk to enter in and harden their hearts to the Lord and push Him away. They are closer to the original design of who we were made to be before so much sin tarnished our ability to shine.

I hope you find freedom in me saying that I believe kids are the easiest group to lead in worship. Let out that exhale and rest in the confirmation that you can do it. I believe in you.

I've led all ages and feel confident to say that six-year-olds are more teachable than eighth graders. I promise, nine-year-olds are easier to lead than a 45 year old man. Even in churches where there has not been an abundance of teaching or vision for this area, kids can still be led in worship. Why? Because, each one of us was wired for it. We all worship something. Whether it's a video game or a job title, a designer label or a popularity contest, humans worship. That's a guarantee that I'd put as much faith in as the reality that the sun is going to rise again tomorrow. The issue of worship is not *if* but what.

Plenty of churches still have their challenges. It may look like a group of kids on the back row trying hard to not engage, and possibly even rolling their eyes. If we were having a one-on-one conversation and I was coaching you through this, I would unpack the three reasons that you are experiencing pushback.

#1 - What have you taught them about worship?

How do you teach them weekly the what, why, where, when, and how of worship? Do you lead like David by telling them why you do it and, most importantly, how to do it?

Have you allowed music to be a time filler or just a fun activity with as much spiritual weight as a game?

Do you wrap your worship sets in prayer and treat the time with reverence as you posture your heart and those you're leading to show honor to the Lord?

When I am leading worship at an event such as a camp or VBS, that first session tells me a lot about what the kids experience on Sundays in their churches. How they respond and engage with me right off the bat tells me where they're at and how little they know about what worship time is truly about. So, I begin drawing a box for them and fill it with an understanding of why we worship and what our posture should look like. I invite them to take a step and session by session, we start walking and they begin engaging. I watch the shift happen. It's amazing how far they can come in only a few services. (The equivalent of a month or more of Sunday services.)

#2 - What does your music sound like?

Song choices, song recordings, and production style can make a huge difference. Evaluate whether it's lame or hokey. We've all heard kids' music that sounds like nails on a chalkboard. Is that what you're currently using? When was the last time you received feedback from others, and a report card of sorts, on the music you're currently using? Do you have kids or teens in your own house? Ask questions, play songs for them, and get feedback. Ask those serving with you for additional insight. We talked more about this in chapter 9.

When was the last time you researched what was new? Do you have other ministry friends you can bounce ideas off of? Ask what songs have been winning for them lately. Search the ministry groups on social media platforms for the threads on music. All it takes is a commitment to spend time researching and pulling up songs to gauge whether or not they'd be right for your group.

Have you been doing the same songs for the past 20 years? Great songs are great songs forever. You can listen to most number one hits and quickly understand how they rose to the top. There's just something special about them. It's the beat, the melody, the lyric, or a combo of all those things. There's something uniquely special and infectious. Relying on past successes is just that. It's not that all old songs are bad, but there is a certain amount of analysis and evaluation that must periodically be factored in to make sure you haven't lost touch on the pulse of your current kids. What do they like? What do they need? What are they responding to? What songs are no longer resonating with them?

Don't be afraid to scrap a song if it's not working. It may have served you well for five years. Guess what? That was worth it. It's OK to let it go or simply give it a rest. Seeking the Lord and using the tools He's given you to gain wisdom on how to lead your kids will never leave you empty-handed.

In seasons where you need to make changes, pruning song choices and planting new ones will be a natural part of the process. You can learn about introducing new songs in chapter 18.

I remember a conversation I had with a group of boys at a

summer camp where I was leading worship. They were hanging out after chapel time, waiting for their turn for lunch. We got into a conversation about music. They asked me what music I listened to and I was trying very hard to give them answers they would find cool, but still be God-honoring. We exchanged our answers and theirs included AC/DC and several other fairly heavy rock-n-roll bands. I walked away from that conversation saddened. Those boys had just shared with me what kind of music they were into, but I knew there was no way that the kids ministry they were encountering on Sunday mornings was meeting the needs of their musical tastes. Even more so, I was pretty confident the leader who brought them to camp was clueless about what these preteen boys were into when it came to their music choices.

I'm not saying that we're trying to mimic the things of this world in how we worship on Sundays. I don't believe the gift we are giving ever changes, but the gift wrap we use can certainly change styles. The presence and relationship of Jesus is the gift. The musical style of the song is the package that we present it in. Make sure your gift is palatable and desirable.

#3 - Who do you have leading them?

Is it a person who older kids would want to be like? Do they respect him or her? Those are two incredibly important ingredients. If you don't have anyone leading them, then that's the first thing I would work fast to change. They need a leader. Someone who can navigate the worship time. They need a model of worship and someone pointing the way, inviting them to join in the song of praise. Without that, they are just going to watch the song video because that's what we do when we're at home. We sit and watch. We don't stand and dance along to it.

Anytime you can get a teenage boy or young man to help you,

that will be a bonus win in gaining the interest of the boys. Although I fully support this as a winning option, if you do not have a guy to help you lead worship, please don't feel like that's a set-up for failure. That's simply not true. I know firsthand that women and girls can lead worship and be incredibly effective. Being a leader is a key ingredient to that. Without leadership, you are just a worship singer. Have a plan for where you're taking them. Being direct and speaking in and with the authority you have been given is another layer.

Most issues you're encountering can be resolved with one or a combination of the three things above.

Differing Palates

I go to a church where there are many Australians on staff. One of the pastors shared about his love for Vegemite. Have you ever had it? It's an Australian food staple. Years ago, I was blessed to be able to go to Melbourne and Sydney, Australia to minister. I distinctly remember the breakfast I had at the hotel the morning after my arrival. I was so excited to try the famous Vegemite I had always heard about. Excited...until I actually tried it. Yuck! I was not impressed. I couldn't comprehend what it was about this savory condiment that the Aussies loved so much.

My pastor shared how it's as common to a kid as our peanut butter and jelly sandwich is. An everyday comfort food of sorts. Everyone grows up with it and seemingly loves it. He went on to share the reason an Australian loves and is drawn to the non-sweet, savory flavor of Vegemite, while the American shrugs it off saying "it's gross," is that their palate was formed to love it. They started eating it when they were young and it's something they have grown up with and learned to love from an early age.

Developing the Palates of Children

I immediately thought of my southern roots and the delicacy that I consider to be boiled peanuts. I was born in Mississippi, lived in Alabama, and am now in Tennessee. If you've ever driven to the beaches of Florida, then you've likely seen them set up at the gas station. Huge pots of this salty goodness. I prefer my boiled peanuts cold, by the way. Those who haven't grown up with this flavor might judge and say "they're slimy" or "they're gross," but not to me. I grew up eating them and it's a food that is considered a treat to me. Why? Because my palate was formed to love it.

We could also discuss our favorite hamburgers and whether you're Team In-N-Out or Team Whataburger, or maybe even Team Five Guys. I'm sure you have an opinion about which one is best. I don't believe all hamburgers should be in the same competition with one another because their styles vary. Sometimes they are independently good. For the record, I'm an In-N-Out girl. In California, their locations have a line for both lunch and dinner. Not many fast food places can say that. I'm convinced it's one of the best meals in the U.S. for the amount of money spent. Likely your opinion was influenced by what you grew up with or by what your parents provided for you. It's the burger that your palate was conditioned to desire.

This got me thinking about our ministries and our times of leading kids in worship. How are we forming palates to love the presence of God? Week in and week out, how are we developing a hunger in our kids to press in and draw close to the Father? Children's ministry works hard to develop a lot of biblical character in kids, as it should. If I'm honest, though, one of the characteristics of a Christ follower that the Church has worked to develop the very least is that of a worshiper. What do you say we change that? I believe the time is now. You are leading for such a time as this. Let's choose to develop palates that love to worship. Let's strategize to develop palates that hunger and crave the things of God in their lives.

Just as an Australian loves their vegemite, a Southerner desires boiled peanuts, and a Californian craves In-N-Out, how much more should the children of God have a palate that is formed to love encounters with His presence?

I truly believe that repetition matters. If you want anything to become a habit, it starts with repeatedly doing the same thing over and over. All performers know this. Whether it's playing an instrument, walking a tightrope, juggling bowling balls, or riding a unicycle. The only way you are going to become a master at those particular things is by practice and repetition. It's not enough to speak a single message on worship and expect that your kids are going to magically get it. Yes, doing a series on worship can be a great launching point. It can even start the process of helping you do the hard work of shifting previous mindsets and softening hearts to be more receptive, but it takes the repeated repetition of things you say and do in order for it to become second nature. Oh how I long for the kids we lead to develop the habit and muscle of being a worshiper. May they be just like David whose automatic reflex was to worship God.

I have people ask me often about what my parents did right. As preacher's kids, my sister and I both grew up in the Church, and still love and diligently serve the Lord. When I reflect on our childhood, what sticks out the most to me was my parents' repetition. There are things that they repeated to us over and over and over. In conversations, in birthday cards, day in and day out. There were phrases they repeated that I honestly didn't think much about, or even agreed to at the time, BUT one day it clicked. I remember when the lightbulb went off that I wanted that character in my life, or that a particular value is important. Yes, that a certain rule is worthy to live by, and on and on. The repetition displayed by my parents pointed me in the direction I should go. They modeled how to get there, until the day I could take myself. Until I wanted and desired those things spiritually.

The Psalmist understood the power of repetition. Take a look at Psalm 136. Every single verse includes the phrase, "His love endures forever." Twenty-six different times he told us the same thing. Why? So we won't forget. That no matter the situation, we would be able to see. Even when the dynamics change and a page is turned in the story. "His love endures forever." The phrase is repeated so we would finally HEAR it after the 10th time, and start to believe it after the 17th time. God's Word has repetition in passages like Psalm 136, but also in the places where the New Testament quotes and references something from the Old Testament. I believe that repetition matters. It makes a difference.

After a farmer plants something, they don't just water the seed once and then walk away until harvest time. It gets watered daily and weekly, again and again, so that growth can happen.

Your kids need experiences to worship, in repetition.

Your kids need lessons of what the heart of a worshiper is, in repetition.

Your kids need understanding and how-to skillsets passed on to them, in repetition.

Your kids need a leader who invites them to sit at the table of the King, in repetition.

Your kids need a leader who tells them how to engage, not just before the song starts but throughout the song and instrumental breaks, in repetition.

Your kids need someone encouraging them and calling them

to the sacrifice of praise, even when they don't think they can do it anymore, in repetition.

A rhythm is a steady beat. It doesn't waver or shift. It doesn't speed up or slow down. There is no autopilot. It requires attention and focus. In a band, you want your drummer to be able to play a consistent tempo, just like a metronome provides. Creating a rhythm of worship discipleship means that you are consistently providing opportunities to take part in worship. You also consistently provide knowledge of why worship matters and an understanding of how to be a worshiper after God's heart. You continually provide intentionality to this area because of the vision that *you* define. Every age group and class in your children's ministry needs a vision for worship defined. It doesn't have to be long. It may be one to three sentences, but what do you want to teach and develop in each age group about worship? Define it. I share much more about this in the Sweet Sound Leader Implementation Guide to help you gain a vision for your kids in the area of worship. Communicate this vision to your volunteer team, as well. The only way the discipleship of worship will happen is if everyone is aware of the goal and is consistently working to lead in a way that will accomplish the goal the vision describes.

Repetition is a part of discipleship. God has been increasingly opening my eyes to see that, as ministry leaders, we have a responsibility to disciple those in our care to be the worshipers He made them to be. When we are in Heaven, I truly believe we will give an account for how we stewarded the opportunities with the young lives we were privileged to shepherd.

One day, I was studying the word discipleship. It led me to a couple words that are from the same family tree. The two words that certainly go hand and hand are *discipline* and *disciple*. Let's take a look at the definitions of these words.

1. *Discipline*
   a. *control gained by enforcing obedience or order*
   b. *orderly or prescribed conduct or pattern of behavior*
   c. *(verb) to train or develop by instruction and exercise especially in self-control...perfecting moral character*
2. *Disciple*
   a. *one who accepts and assists in spreading the doctrines of another*
   b. *one of the twelve in the inner circle of Christ's followers according to the Gospel accounts*

There's truth and application for us in every one of those definitions. Some of the things that stick out to me are: order, pattern, perfecting moral character, spreading doctrine (truth and knowledge), and being in the inner circle. I'd be shocked to find a leader who wouldn't admit to having a desire for those they lead to find their place in the inner circle of the Lord. Just stop right now and get a vision of the kids who you lead, sitting at the feet of Jesus. That's the ultimate place we want to lead them to. So, what steps do you need to start taking in order to ensure they get there?

It is time to STOP just DOING songs and START LEADING worship!

When you truly lead and disciple through worship, it means they are going to know how to get there. They are going to long to sit at His feet. They are fully aware of the beautiful exchange that comes from giving our worship and receiving the comfort and holiness of

God's presence. There is nothing like it.

Think about your invitations to worship. How are you developing their palates to crave the seasonings and flavors that worship provides? The Psalms tell us to taste and see that He is good. How are you creating space for kids to experience the goodness of who God is? In a dry and weary land, how are you allowing the presence of God to saturate and quench the thirst of the kids you are ministering to? Do they know that He is like a cool cup of water on a hot summer day? He is all they need. He is what they need. Waiting until they are a teenager or an adult to learn this is not an option. In most cases, it's too late. *Now* is the time.

We are living in a crazy world. Now more than ever, I believe our kids need a hiding place that can only be found in God's presence. Teach them week by week, song by song, why they were created to worship. Show them how to express their worship by modeling it and leading them with repetition. Help them long to sit at His feet. Tell them their worship is a sweet sound in God's ear. Let them encounter who God is by creating space for them to know Him by singing songs full of the Word and character of God. Let them experience that there's nothing like His presence. Most of all, prayerfully consider how you can form their palate to hunger for the things of God. "Go and make disciples." Those aren't my words, but the words of the One who sent me.

Quantity

Doesn't Matter

When I am speaking with or coaching other leaders, I often get asked the question, "How many songs should you do each week?" There is not a "one size fits all" answer, and here's why. Every church leader has a different amount of time to work with that they need to fill. Some churches have hour-long services. Others have services that last for two hours or more. Some kids ministries only have 30 minutes of large group time because they spend the remainder of the time in small groups. So, I can't give you a firm number of songs that you should be doing because everyone has different factors of time and restraints they are dealing with.

The most common number I hear among churches is three songs. I've had conversations with some leaders who can only do two, while others have space to do five. There is nothing in the Bible telling us how many songs to sing in worship. We are simply commanded to sing out in worship. You have to consider the minutes you have, the various elements you want to include, and then seek the Lord for how to spend those minutes wisely when you gather.

I believe very strongly that how you place the songs is one of the most crucial elements. I've experienced some children's ministries that place each song individually. Here's an example:

> **Kick-off Song**
> Game
> **Praise Song**
> Memory Verse
> Offering
> **Worship Song**
> Message
> Response time

As a worship leader, I will confess to you that this layout is hard. It may be great on attention spans, (and those must be considered for the various ages you're leading) but you won't be able to build any momentum with the constant starting and stopping. You're also wasting some time in the transition of getting everyone on their feet and then sitting back down. And, transitioning from one person on stage to another. Did I mention that it's hard?

Have you ever been driving somewhere and you end up catching every single traffic light? Did that annoy you? Think about it for a minute. It's likely that the journey took you longer than it normally would with the extra slowdowns involved. Your lack of patience possibly became irritated with all the stopping and starting again. Accelerate and decelerate. Accelerate and decelerate. Well, this is what it's like as a worship leader to have three songs separated. It may have taken the first 90-120 seconds of a three-minute song to get everyone involved and focused. If that all ends in another 60 seconds and their focus is redirected to another thing, then you aren't building any momentum. You're distracting them with something completely different. Plus, you're certainly unable to benefit from any momentum that was created transitioning into the next song. When it's time for the next song, they aren't going to pick up where they left off. You'll have to start all over, back at square one. Getting them back up on their feet, saying something inspiring to encourage them to sing out, and most of all, focus on the Lord.

Instead, use that momentum to work FOR you rather than against you. Capitalize on the progress that was made by continuing on with another opportunity to express their worship. Transition to another song.

In the case of a three-song set, my recommendation most weeks is going to be to put two of those songs together. Here are a few examples:

> **2 Praise Songs**
> Other elements of your service
> **1 Worship Song**

> **1 Kick-off Song**
> Other elements of your service
> **2 Praise & Worship Songs**

> **1 Praise Song**
> Other elements of your service
> **2 Worship Songs**

Just to be clear, I do believe that attention spans are important and should be considered. If you have time for five songs every week, that's amazing! But, you most likely will not want all five of those in one spot. Your sets may look like the following:

2 Praise Songs
Other elements of your service
1 Praise Song
Other elements of your service
2 Worship Songs

1 Kick-off Song
Other elements of your service
2 Praise Songs
Other elements of your service
2 Worship Songs

1 Kick-off Song
Other elements of your service
3 Praise & Worship Songs
Other elements of your service
1 Response Worship Song

2 Praise Songs
Other elements of your service
3 Praise & Worship Songs

As you may have noticed in the examples I gave, I believe that service orders shouldn't be the same every week. I do realize that preschool kids love routine and familiarity. If the same format every week works best for your preschoolers, then continue with that. However, if we're talking about preteen and elementary age children, don't fall prey to being predictable. Keep things fun and interesting. Don't let them know or be able to predict what is happening next.

When they know what's happening next, then it's much easier for them to pick and choose prioritizing in their minds what their engagement level is going to be. That may actually work against you in gaining the level of participation you would like. They may be holding out on this thing that's gonna happen in 10 minutes rather than jumping in with both feet right now. There's a lesson in that for us all. By changing up your format, you remain in control. Plus, it keeps things interesting for everybody: kids, team leaders, and volunteers, included.

I also would encourage you to mix things up. Again, let's sacrifice being predictable. In worship leading, you have various tools at your disposal, but the tool of predictability is one that's better left behind. If you frequently do three songs in a service, then occasionally do four songs and surprise them. Or, one week only do two. For those who normally hold out until song three because they think it's not important for them to participate, or they are waiting for the grand finale, they will miss out. However, in future weeks, they may be more prone to engage earlier in the worship time so they don't forfeit that opportunity again.

My dad came up with five standard service orders and then rotated those around each week of every month. The rotation was naturally built to circle around without the hard work of analyzing how to change things up every single week. There was a week one schedule, week two schedule, and so on. Find a system that works for you. Maybe your changes fall more monthly or quarterly. Come up with a structure that will take some of the busy work out and always, always remember that you have the authority to change things as needed. Most of all, be responsive to how the Spirit leads you to plan and prepare for that particular service. In songwriting, there is a rule that says: "You have to know the rules to break the rules." I believe that applies to this conversation here.

We do have access to help and wisdom.

"For those who are led by the Spirit of God are the children of God." - Romans 8:14

We are creative people because we were made in the image of a Creator God.

"In the beginning God created the heavens and the earth." - Genesis 1:1

"So God created mankind in his own image, in the image of God he created them." - Genesis 1:27

We must never forfeit that still small voice that is our helper.

"But when he, the Spirit of truth, comes, he will guide you into all the truth. He will not speak on his own; he will speak only what he hears, and he will tell you what is yet to come. He will glorify me because it is from me that he will receive what he will make known to you." - John 16:13-14

Holy Spirit wants to help us plan the best, every single week, for our kids. Be sensitive to His voice. Stop, listen, and most certainly follow with obedience.

You may feel like a team of one, but you are never only a team of one. You may be one person in the physical, but the Trinity is with you. They will help and guide you, but you have to invite them into your space. When you sit down to plan a worship set, it would benefit you to spend some time in prayer and worship. Turn on a song and plug in headphones, if needed. Turn off all the alarms and warning message sounds on your phone and computer. Direct your own heart to focus on the greatness of God. Draw close and invite the Lord to lead and guide you in how to serve your kids. What type of song do they need on this particular day?

It feels so elementary to remind church leaders to pray about their decisions, but I'll be honest, I've been guilty of being so focused on a physical need that I forgot to pray about it. I remember one day while on staff at the church, I was in my worship pastor's office. We were making a list of new equipment that we needed to purchase. We also made a list of some various musician roles that we needed to fill. After we made the list, my worship pastor said, "Let's pray about it." I remember thinking, *"Well, that's brilliant!"* In all the chaos of leading and organizing teams, I honestly forgot that I could ask God to help and He would answer my prayer. So, don't make the same mistake I did. Seek God's help because He has promised if we seek Him, we will find Him. He cares about what you are doing and He wants to help you. He is a gentleman, though, and is waiting for you to ask first.

Let's talk about another challenge in song set length for those of you who are very limited on large group time. I've heard from many leaders who only have time for two songs. They question what to choose and how to obtain more in the experience they can offer their kids with such limited time at play. In this type of scenario, I would encourage you to choose different types of songs from week to week. You can't check off all the boxes in one week with only one or two slots. But, throughout one month, you could help your kids experience an engaging activity song as a kick-off. A praise song that helps them to celebrate. Another week, you invite them to posture their hearts in surrender through a slower song of worship. The next week, you lead them in a fun, kid-friendly arrangement of a hymn. Maybe even share the story behind the song and how many hundreds of years it's been sung. At some point, you may have a song that really connects well to what you're teaching and reinforces that message even more.

Don't feel restricted by the limited time. Instead, put on your hat of creativity (because you are made in the image of Creator) and consider what song will help you accomplish what you need to accomplish on that particular day. As I plan a worship set, I consider what's been done in recent weeks and months. What needs to be revisited? What song needs a rest? In this situation of limited time, if in the past couple weeks you only did uptempo songs, then it may be time to lead them in a slower worship song. If you led them in a response worship song after a message time in the previous week, then this week might be the right one for a fun, activity song kick-off to get the whole room moving.

Another idea for those with limited time is to consider how you can utilize the travel time to and from a large group. Could you do an additional song as they are dismissed? Maybe it happens as parents are coming into the room to pick them up. Sure, the child may only hear one minute of it and not be there for the entire song, but that is one extra minute that they heard a song full of truth. That is one additional minute where they were able to respond to the Lord with their gifts of worship. If your kids are traveling from another area, such as age-level classrooms or small groups, what if you did a song as they entered the large group room? Lead them in a song as they enter the room. Yes, one class of kids could be there for most of the song while another group comes in during the last thirty seconds, but if it provided even half your kids with the additional time to experience worship, then wouldn't it be worth it?

Remember: Limited time does not have to be a handicap. It simply requires more intentionality in what you do and how you do it.

Building
Intentional
Worship Sets

Chapter Thirteen

Worship sets are journeys. As a leader, you function a bit like a tour guide or cruise director. Just as you wouldn't get on a ship without knowing where it's headed, your congregation is trusting that you have a plan for your service. I believe it is crucial and necessary for you to have a plan for where you are taking your church. When you travel somewhere, you likely use some form of navigation. When I was growing up, that was often a paper map or even travel books from AAA. Nowadays, it's likely that anyone with a smartphone is using navigation to get them from point A to point B. This navigation leads you turn by turn on what path to take, even avoiding a traffic crisis or accident that may alter the route, at times. The only way navigation can work is to identify where you are and where you are wanting to go.

As a worship leader, I have a plan for where I'm headed and how we're gonna get there. The process is tied to song choices and how those specific song choices will lead and move us along on the journey. I identify where my group is in their knowledge and understanding of worship. I determine what I'm going to share that will encourage them to take the next step in their worship. It could be based on a scripture from God's Word. It could be from a lesson learned or revelation God revealed to me. Sometimes as I rehearse, I get an overwhelming sense that I need to share or say something specific as I transition from songs.

The more experience you get, the more confident you can become. But there's also more room for you to rely on past worship sets or clever things said simply because they worked in the past. As your physical abilities increase in leading, you run the risk of leading on autopilot. You may be able to physically ride a bike with your eyes closed, but the problem is you can't see where you're going and a crash is inevitable due to your lack of vision. Unless you're in the middle of nowhere on an open prairie that goes on for many miles, it is inevitable that you will hit something and fall. The fall could be painful and even embarrassing. Just because you can doesn't mean you should.

I believe as you prayerfully plan and as you diligently rehearse so you are better prepared to lead each worship set, God will spotlight exactly what you need to do and share. You can't lead others to a place that you don't know how to get to first. If you're winging it or flying by the seat of your pants, you may survive, but the time might not be as fruitful as if you had pre-determined the vision of where you were taking them. Don't drive aimlessly, but rather, drive intentionally with a desired outcome of where your journey will ultimately lead you.

There are always times where a change of course is needed. It could be their personalities that day. Periodically, it seems everyone is just in a weird mood. Shake those days off. If the next week everything is normal again, then don't change course because of the one "off day." I blame those on barometric pressure or something in the air. They just randomly happen. Don't abandon every song you do or who you have leading solely based on one shaky week.

There are other times where the Spirit moves in a new direction. Does that mean you missed God earlier in the week as you prepared?

I don't believe so. I don't think it's that simple. Maybe the person who showed up that day is going through a tough time and needs God to meet them where they are. Just like when we're traveling in cars, or even on a plane, and we have to avoid certain things while, at times, locating a different path. I've been on many airplanes that had to change their course due to a new weather pattern or condition that wasn't in the original plan. Thankfully we still arrived where we were intending to go, but the path had to change. That's where autopilot will lead you to a crash, and why it's crucial to be sensitive to that nudge from God. You might wonder what that looks like. For me, I could be in the middle of a song and get a sense that I need to say something specific or even start leading the chorus of a song that wasn't planned. I'll be honest and admit that there are times I've attempted to avoid that nudge because it wasn't in the plan, thinking that the rest of the team isn't aware or prepared for the set to be different. But as I try to move forward, I continue to get the sense that I need to say that one thing or sing that other song. If I can't shake the feeling, then I realize that if I don't proceed I will be walking in disobedience. (Insert some tension-filled music from a dramatic movie scene to intensify what you're watching unfold). I do not want to disobey the Lord, so I determine to move forward with what He's asking me to do. You'll never regret being obedient to God. As Eddie DeGarmo, a CCM legend I greatly respect, said: "Success is obedience."

Your set is also like a roller coaster. There should be highs and lows. This is where different types of songs come into play. If the roller coaster was one level and just went around in a circle repeatedly, it would honestly be a pretty boring ride. I've seen some kiddie rides at the fair that did not provide much of a thrill. They just went around and around and never did anything exciting. What makes the experience an adventure and amplifies the fun is found in the highs and lows, ups and downs, twists and turns. Different types of songs. Different tempos of music. Different sounds and genres of songs. All of them are needed and key ingredients to building intentional worship sets. Some songs engage action. Other songs engage the heart. Others bring us to the altar where we can respond in reverence to the One who paid the greatest price and gifted us with His love and mercy. Every one of them is needed. Some songs work great because they are super popular and everyone is drawn to them. Cue those worship songs of the moment that everyone is singing at every church and event you go to, or so it seems! Those songs have a place and purpose. However, there are other songs I use that no one in the room might know, but the message is important. There's something simple and approachable in the lyrics that I believe is a prayer we need to pray as we sing the words over our lives, but more importantly about how great our God is. Those songs also have a place. Some songs I choose because they naturally lead themselves. They encourage the participant to join in based on a lyric that invites them to take part and, most of all, move in action. They can serve as a great kick-off or welcome song. Consider them the greeting in a letter. It's just a warm-up for what's to come. Those songs have a place, too. With some songs, the win is that they put the message of what you're teaching to music. Music is sticky. It stays with us for years and decades to come. So, whether it be a story song or a scripture song, or something else, the best way to get your kids to really remember what you're teaching is to write it on their hearts using the glue that is music, so it will stick forever!

A chef understands how ingredients work together to make a tasty dish.

A dietician understands how nutrition and metabolism work to make our bodies healthier.

A personal trainer is aware of how a specific exercise works and engages certain muscles. The right combination of exercises makes all the difference in a great workout. Your form and the amount of reps you specifically do will determine if it was difficult or not. Will it be a difference maker or was it too easy and attainable?

An artist is aware of how different brushes, types of paint, and the right tools create different outcomes on a canvas.

A worship leader chooses their songs wisely knowing that each one will lead the congregation another step on the journey of running to the Father.

The thrill of a roller coaster is how it transitions from high highs to low lows. The same example can apply in worship. Maybe you've been to a worship night where you experienced something like this, or even vice versa. They may have gone from a super intimate, more serious worship time, and then transitioned into an uptempo song to respond in celebration. In a concert, it's the difference between an artist being on stage playing a song by themselves while everyone shines the flashlight off their phone versus the finale closer that drops confetti on the audience or the performer flying around the arena with some hydraulics (or maybe even pyrotechnics are launched). Highs and lows.

I've also learned that going from an active, uptempo song to something more serious, slower, and worshipful works great for kids. This even works really well with preschoolers. We know that attention spans are important. But a change due to attention span doesn't necessarily mean that it has to be a totally different service element. The change needed could be accomplished by the type of response that song yields.

Building Intentional Worship Sets

If your group is learning the concept of worship and how to participate in a slower worship song, it may work well to surround that song with something fun and active that honestly will make them a little tired. Think of your biggest calorie burner here. Then transition, maybe even allowing them to sit as you sing the song, before you invite them to be still and focus on a more calm moment. This will be more effective than if you had placed that song choice after an element where they were a little more stir crazy.

Side note: I wouldn't normally encourage sitters during worship, but I think it's a step in the process. If they are super young, then it's a way to start them out on solid foods. Think of how a baby begins eating solid foods in puree form before eating tiny, non-choke hazard pieces. Then, after conquering those two things, they can graduate to normal bites of solid food. I have used this same method in leading preschool kids in worship. Yes, they can handle slow songs. I've also used this as a starting point for a group of elementary kids that has no concept of worship beyond action-filled songs. Use your judgment accordingly for your situation and flock you lead.

It's important to analyze your songs and understand what each one accomplishes. Maybe you even categorize your songs. This may make the song planning process easier if you first identify three to five categories of types of songs you can utilize. Determine which category each of these songs fit best into. Make a spreadsheet or index card system with your song catalog and, as you seek to plan and program various elements of your service, make decisions from your various categories that will work best for your desired outcome.

I'm going to share some worship sets with you from events I've done. You'll see why I chose the songs, set order, and repetition of the songs throughout these week-long events.

Sweet Sound

These sets were from a 4-day camp for preteens.

Set 1 - AM

"Trust & Believe" (This served as a theme song for the week, so we kicked off with it)

"Super Wonderful" (Taught them something new, but super engaging and easy)

"Our God" (Something worshipful and familiar)

Set 2 - PM

"Happy & You Know It" (Super engaging and active. The lyrics dictate how to engage)

"There is Power" (Worship, but still a song that's mid tempo and driving)

"We Believe" (A worshipful and familiar "home run" song)

Set 3 - AM

"Trust & Believe" (Theme song repetition)

"Strength & Shield" (Uptemo, active, based on scripture, and easy to follow along even when unfamiliar)

"Glory To Your Name" (Talk about David's heart for worship; based on scripture, worshipful, and new but easy to catch on to)

Set 4 - PM

"Super Wonderful" (Uptempo, active and engaging, repetition from another day, "home run" type song)

"Who You Say I Am" (Familiar worship song; tied into message)

"Good Good Father" (Familiar worship song, but took a moment to encourage them to take a step in their worship.

Drawing close to the Father)

Set 5 - AM
"Strength & Shield" (Uptempo, active and engaging, repetition from another day)
"Not Ashamed" (Uptempo, the whole crowd participates on a key phrase, teaches them something new, but yet everyone can engage the first time)
"What A Beautiful Name" (Familiar worship song; invitation to worship)

Set 6 - PM
"Trust & Believe" (Theme song repetition)
"Glory To Your Name" (Worship song repetition)
"Who You Say I Am" (Familiar worship song that ties into message)

Set 7 - AM
"Trust & Believe" (Theme song repetition)
"Not Ashamed" (Praise song repetition; engages the whole crowd)
"Glory To Your Name" (Worship song repetition. This one has fully connected now and it's oh so sweet!)

Set 8 - PM
"Super Wonderful" (Praise song repetition. Engages the whole crowd. "Home run" song)
"What A Beautiful Name" (Worship song repetition)
"Oceans" (Familiar "home run" worship song. Ties into

message; Invitation to trust)

These sets were from a 5-day VBS for Preschoolers.

Day 1

"Praise the Lord Every Day" (Uptempo and super active. Lyrics dictate what to do)

"Hosanna Rock" (Uptempo, "Home run" song)

"The B-I-B-L-E" (It's VBS, so we have to do The B-I-B-L-E! Plus, it's a classic)

Other programming elements

"I Like To" (Uptempo and super active. Lyrics dictate what to do)

"Super Wonderful" (Super heroes, uptempo, easy to engage everyone)

"Father Abraham" (An active song that's also a classic)

Day 2

"Brand New Day" (Lyrically a great kick off; engages the crowd by the lyrics)

"If You're Happy & You Know It" (Familiar, active, a classic)

"Super Wonderful" (Repetition from previous day. A "home run" that engages everyone)

Other programming elements

"My Best Friend" (Includes the days of the week, educational, and super easy to catch on to)

"God Is So Good" (A simple song of worship, easy, and a classic)

"My God Is Number One" (Another superhero song that's also educational and includes counting. Active and engaging)

Day 3

"Praise the Lord Every Day" (Repetition from a previous day. Uptemo, super active. Lyrics dictate what to do)

"My God Is Number One" (Repetition from a previous day. Educational, active and engaging)

"Hosanna Rock" (Uptempo, "home run" song)

Other programming elements

"My Best Friend" (Repetition from a previous day, educational, and easy)

"How Great Is Our God" (Invitation to worship. Familiar "home run" song)

"The B-I-B-L-E" (Repetition from a previous day, classic song, it's VBS and about the Bible)

Day 4

"Hosanna Rock" (Uptemo, "home run" song)

"I Like To" (Repetition from a previous day. Uptempo and super active. Lyrics dictate what to do)

"One, Two, Three" (Uptempo and an easy song to engage. Ties into salvation message day)

Other programming elements

"Stop & Go" (Teach something new that's uptempo, FUN, and engaging)

"I Love You Lord" (Worshipful and a classic)

"Super Wonderful" (Repetition from a previous day, engaging, active, and a "home run" song)

Day 5

"I Like To" (Repetition from a previous day. Uptempo and super active. Lyrics dictate what to do)

"One, Two, Three" (Repetition from previous day. Uptempo and an easy song to engage)

"Stop & Go" (Repetition from a previous day. Uptemo, fun and engaging)

Other programming elements

"Hosanna Rock" (Repetition from a previous day, uptempo and "home run" song)

"Shout" (Teach them something new, midtempo, has a call and repeat section to engage everyone)

"Super Wonderful" (Repetition from a previous day, active and a "home run" song. End on a high note of engagement!)

These sets were from a 4-day camp for elementary ages.

Day 1 - AM

"Happy and You Know It" (Super engaging and active. The lyrics dictate how to engage)

"Not Ashamed" (Uptempo, the whole crowd participates on a key phrase, teaches them something new, yet everyone can engage for the first time)

"Better Than the Best Thing" (Uptempo. Taught something new. Has a simple "oh" vamp section making it easy for everyone to participate)

Other programming elements

"Our God" (Midtempo, familiar praise song)

"Better Than the Best Thing" (Uptempo closer. Repeated from earlier in the set to help them catch on and cause it to stick, as they are dismissed from the session.)

Building Intentional Worship Sets

Day 1 - PM

"Not Ashamed" (Repetition from morning, uptempo, engages the whole crowd)

"Super Wonderful" (Taught them something new, but super engaging and easy)

"Strength & Shield" (Scriptural, engaging, and easy to catch on to)

Other programming elements

"We Believe" (Familiar "home run" worship song)

"Who You Say I Am" (Familiar "home run" worship song, important confession, ties into theme)

Day 2 - AM

"Happy and You Know It" (Repetition from previous day, super active and engaging to wake them up)

"Hosanna Rock" (This is a "home run" song geared for the younger kids, but it's active and engages everyone)

"Strength & Shield" (Repetition from previous day, uptempo, scriptural, engages everyone)

Other programming elements

"We Believe" (Repetition from previous day, familiar, "home run" song)

"10,000 Reasons" (Worshipful, familiar "home run" song. Appropriate in the morning based on the lyrics)

Day 2 - PM

"Not Ashamed" (Repetition from previous day, uptempo, engages the whole crowd)

"Super Wonderful" (Repetition from previous day, "home

run" song)

"There Is Power" (Midtempo, driving praise song)

Other programming elements

"Who You Say I Am" (Repetition from previous day, familiar "home run" worship song, important confession, ties into theme)

"Good Good Father" (Invitation to take a step and draw close to the Father. Familiar worship song)

Day 3 - AM

"Praise the Lord Every Day" (Fun, active, and engaging in the lyric to get everyone involved, although the song is geared for younger children)

"Super Wonderful" (Repetition from previous day, "home run" song)

"Glory To Your Name" (Teach them a new worship song, scripture based, easy to learn)

Other programming elements

"Forever & Ever" (Crowd engagement is FUN! Get kids on stage. Has a part for everyone to get involved in)

"Our God" (Mid-tempo, familiar worship song)

Day 3 - PM

"Not Ashamed" (Repetition from previous day, uptempo, engages the whole crowd)

"Better Than the Best Thing" (Repetition from a previous day. Has an easy "oh" vamp section making it easy for everyone to participate)

"Who You Say I Am" (Repetition from a previous day. Familiar "home run" worship song)

Other programming elements
"Glory To Your Name" (Repetition from a previous session. Worship, scriptural; Starting to catch on well)
"What A Beautiful Name" (Worshipful, "home run" familiar song)

Day 4 - AM
"Happy and You Know It" (Repetition from previous day, super active and engaging to wake them up)
"Alive" (Familiar, uptempo praise song)
"Hosanna Rock" (Intentionally engaging the youngest children, but still provides an invitation for all to be involved with a "home run" song)
Other programming elements
"Oceans" (Familiar worship song. This song has a special anointing on it. It's a "home run" song with any age, even defying logic of what components make a great worship song for children)
"Better Than the Best Thing" (Repetition from a previous day. Has an easy "oh" vamp section making it easy for everyone to participate as they are dismissed)

Day 4 - PM
"Strength & Shield" (Repetition from previous day, uptempo, scriptural, engages everyone)
"Super Wonderful" (Repetition from previous day, "home run" song)
"There Is Power" (Repetition from previous day, midtempo, driving praise song)

Other programming elements
"What A Beautiful Name" (Repetition from previous day, familiar "home run" worship song)
"Who You Say I Am" (Repetition from previous day, familiar "home run" worship song, important confession, ties into theme)
Message
Salvation altar call
"I Love You" (Worship song about the cross, easy to catch on to, appropriate for the invitation)

Whether you're planning a multi-day summer event, weekly services, or a special worship night, consider what is being taught and the minutes you have to fill. Find the balance between new, familiar, active, worshipful, and fan-favorites that everyone will engage with. Want to jumpstart the moment? Find a song that lyrically directs and calls for the engagement. Create highs and lows because both are needed. Often your sets will go high energy to slow, but mix it up and purposefully end up-tempo from time to time. Give invitations to invite them into times of worship. Help them understand what a next step looks like and why their gift of worship matters to the Lord. Tie into themes that are being taught. Reinforce the message with a song that will make it stick for years to come.

When I sit down to plan, I reference the past month or two of worship sets. What needs to be repeated because it's newer? What have you not sung in a month? What have you not sung for a couple months that you need to bring back? What songs do you have that tie into what's being taught? What new songs are you needing to introduce? Pray and ask the Holy Spirit to give you peace and show you where to place each song. Where have engagements and action just bought you the change in your pocket to then have a teaching moment or invite them to learn a new song? Use the knowledge that you have learned. Consider the track record of what's been working and what hasn't. Keep a spreadsheet of the sets you plan so you can easily access them as you're looking at upcoming sets. As I plan the songs, I listen to the Spirit. Where do I feel peace? What songs or spots do I feel tension or an unsettling feeling? Maybe those aren't right. Try something else in its place. Did you experience peace? Create a habit of saying, "Spirit, lead me." I believe God is always speaking to us. We're just not always the best listeners. Choose to listen and obey. The more you do it, the easier it will become to develop those spiritual muscles that will build intentional worship sets to impact the hearts of those who you lead in worship.

Let Me Introduce
You to a
New Song

Chapter Fourteen

It is so easy to rely on former successes and what has worked well for us in the past that we forget to inject our sets with some new songs. I think there are many reasons for that. It takes time to research and find new songs that are a good fit for your group. Every church has a personality and a DNA that is uniquely theirs. Sometimes a song that everyone else is doing isn't the right fit for your group. That's OK. Do not fall victim to song choice peer pressure. There have been popular songs in other churches that fell flat in mine, but other times where a lesser known song was a total win. I believe it's important to learn your church culture and what works for your people. You should lead and steward them well. Sometimes that looks like saying "yes" to a song and, on other occasions, it means it's a "no." Both are acceptable. I've experienced songs that I personally loved and were a blast for our youth band to play. The only issue was that the song didn't connect with our students so I had to be okay with just listening to it in my car or jamming out with the band when we had a few extra minutes. But to keep placing the song in our worship sets wasn't serving our kids well.

Set aside time once a quarter to analyze what *is* working well. What is it about those particular songs that your students are responding to? Is it message, music, style, or action? Try to determine *why* they are winning. If you're still unsure, consider asking others so you can gain additional insight. The more you can learn why it's working, the more you can use that powerful knowledge in future song choice decision making. Also consider what isn't working so well. Maybe it's a song that was everyone's favorite in the past, but it's now outgrown your peoples' tastes. You need to be aware of that so you can place it in sets accordingly. Most songs seem to serve us for seasons. Knowledge is power. Use it well.

I know that both time and budget are needed to introduce new songs in your ministry. Neither thing may be convenient. It will not only require time to research and find new songs, but it will also require time for your leaders and teams to practice and prepare, learning the songs so they can be led well. In addition, there is an expense to purchase music and videos for use in your ministry. You need to make sure you are using music ethically in your church and that will require funds, but so do the TV's and sound systems in your classrooms, as well as the goldfish crackers or veggie straws you serve at snack time. Each of these are necessary and serve a purpose. The same is true for music and video that give you the group viewing permissions for classrooms. You may also need special licensing to provide content via live streams and on social media to families. Do your research. Send emails to ask questions. Just as you're trying to be a good steward of what has been entrusted to you, content creators, songwriters, video producers, and the like are also trying to steward what God has given them through the form of talent and investment they've made creating media that will benefit your ministry. Support them well. In doing so, God will honor you and bless your ministry. As we minister, let's walk in integrity on stage and off. Doing things the right way helps model integrity to those who you personally get the privilege of impacting. I believe God is glorified through that process. Yes, these are all line items in your budget, but I believe the small financial investment it costs versus the spiritual growth it enables is truly "priceless," in the words of the old Mastercard commercials.

When was the last time you introduced something new? Was it at VBS last year? Maybe it was at camp. Have you been relying on the same songs that have worked well for the past five, seven, or ten years? It may be past time for a new song.

Let me say that I believe there is always a core group of songs that stand the test of time. There's a reason we've been singing songs like "Father Abraham" and "This Little Light Of Mine" for generations. In the adult world, an example would be classic hymns like "Amazing Grace" or "It Is Well." They are still relevant messages and cherished by many. But if you sang these songs every week, people would become numb to them and, therefore, they would be less impactful. I certainly don't want anyone to stop singing my "Hosanna Rock" anytime soon. There are some songs that are able to be sustained for years or even decades, and there's beauty in that. I have noticed that some songs often win for a season of time. That season may be a longer stretch or it may be a shorter length of time, but neither one is forever. Even in my own music catalog, I have songs that I released when I first began making music for kids that were super popular for years. Those songs would be the most requested and expected from me when I performed live. But as time has shifted (and let's admit, those preteens I wrote the song for are now young adults, college graduates, and married with kids), I understand that not every song serves all generations of a demographic, indefinitely. And that's OK. It doesn't make that song bad. It doesn't make that song unsuccessful. The song still has a place.

It accomplished a lot of good over the years. It's just not a number one favorite forever. Just as the radio charts change over the years, so does your kids worship playlist.

I'm not saying every single song you sing must be new or something you introduced in the past year. However, I am encouraging you to make sure that you choose to periodically add something new to the mix. That may be one new song a month. It could mean a new song every quarter. I think a lot of that is determined by how many songs per week you're doing in the first place. The fewer the overall amount of songs you're using, the fewer spots you have for something new. In comparison, if you're able to do more songs per week, then you can also teach more new songs because you have so many more choices to fill. The ratio of new versus familiar rules in favor of the latter. It makes the unfamiliar new song carry a smaller risk.

I love backing things up with the Word of God because His Word is what matters, not my own experience or opinion. Let's take another look at one of the lessons we learned from David: The importance of singing new songs to the Lord. David sang in Psalm 40:3, "He put a new song in my mouth, a hymn of praise to our God. Many will see and fear the Lord and put their trust in him."

And yet again, in Psalm 98:1: *"Sing to the Lord a new song, for he has done marvelous things." (Fun fact! Did you know that "Joy to the World" was Isaac Watts' lyrical adaptation of Psalm 98?)*

Now, we'll say it again for the people in the back! Psalm 149:1 reiterates, "Praise the Lord. Sing to the Lord a new song, his praise in the assembly of his faithful people."

David wasn't the only one to signify the importance of our new song. Take a look at Isaiah 42:10: "Sing to the Lord a new song, his praise from the ends of the earth." Isaiah talks about new things coming forth in both Isaiah 42 and 43. One thing I am certain of, if you want to see God move in new ways in your life, your song of praise will be required. Even in this passage, Isaiah is encouraging us to stir ourselves up with a **NEW** song to the Lord. Amen!

Let me shift to the practical side of introducing new songs:

1. Introduce it as a new song. It is perfectly okay to "let the cat out the bag," as they say, and share that "We have a new song to sing together today. It's called *"insert title."* It's all about *"whatever the song is about."* Singalong with me as you catch on to it. Let's go!"

2. Place it on a pre-service music playlist weeks and months ahead of time. Let the song become familiar to your kids without ever introducing it during your services. It will get into their subconscious and when it's time to introduce it during service time, they will think it sounds familiar, like they have heard it before. That way, you are not starting from square one.

This tip can also apply to special summer events or throughout the year where you may have many new songs to teach them. Start allowing those songs to be heard in the weeks and months leading up to the event, playing in the background on pre-service and hallway playlists, and potentially on playlists you make for families to access on music streaming platforms. (More on that in chapter 21.)

3. For the first couple of times, find a way to do the song more than once. Unfortunately, since we know that we don't see all of our kids every single

week, be aware that it may be a few weeks before a child is back to experience the new song. This means it takes that much longer for new songs to become familiar and second nature to all of your kids. I suggest finding a way to include it a second time. Maybe that looks like leading the song again as the class is dismissed and parents are picking up their kids from the room. Some kids may hear it for another minute, but other children could experience the full song. It's like a double helping. It's a worthy use of time to keep the song in their ears and become more and more familiar to them. It all comes down to using your time wisely and efficiently. You could lead the song again live, or you could just play the audio or show the video. Whoever is hosting or helping lead the pickup time could even encourage the kids to "sing along to the new song" periodically. The idea here is to play it again. Use the recurrence of the extra play to your advantage.

4. Before you introduce a new song, try teaching just the chorus. It could be done acapella or with one instrument. If you play guitar or another instrument, play it while you teach only the chorus. Any key part or phrase of the song you expect them to catch on to quickest will work great in this method.

Last but not least, my number one tip for how to lead new songs is:

5. Surround new songs with a "home run" song. What is a "home run" song, you ask? A home run song is

a song that I identify as a win every single time. It could be one of the kids' favorites. It may even be a popular hit worship song of the year type chorus that everyone really joins in well with. I am always going to surround the new song I'm introducing with a home run song which could look like:

1. Home Run Song
2. New Song

   or

1. New Song
2. Home Run Song

I do this because I don't want to push away those who are less inclined to sing along the first time out. I don't want to disengage them for any length of time longer than I have to. Let's face it: some people won't even try to sing along until they feel comfortable with the new song. By surrounding the new territory with a "home run" song, I'm getting them involved to the fullest capacity as quickly as I can. Or, I'm hoping some of the excitement of their favorite song will inspire them to try the new song a little quicker. No matter what, I made sure within my set that I had them fully participating on the home run song even if the one I'm introducing feels like a sacrifice in the current moment.

Set aside time to identify what your home run songs are. Don't plan a set with all of your home run songs in one day. (Well, you could do that for a special worship night.) Instead, place them *strategically* in your weekly sets when you want to accelerate participation.

When I introduce a new song, I always repeat it a couple weeks in a row. Then, I take a week off. Follow up by placing it in the set again on week four. The next month, I include it every other week until it feels like everyone has caught on. You can then move it into a normal rotation. So how long does it really take to introduce a new song? At least a couple months.

Sometimes you go through the process of introducing a new song and it just doesn't pay off. I try to be really confident in a song before I introduce it. At times, it's a no-brainer. On some occasions, I pull in other leaders on our team and see what they think. But even through those various rounds of vetting a song, some still fall flat. If it's not the right fit, you don't have to force it. There is no "new song police" that's gonna show up on your doorstep and ticket you for discontinuing use of a song that didn't work well for your group. You can still utilize the song on your pre-service playlists. You could still recommend it as a song for families to listen and jam out to. But, don't be afraid to lay down the baggage of what's not working so you can pick up something new that will.

What, Why, Where, When and How

"We don't do slow songs because our kids don't know how to respond to them."

I can't tell you how many times I've heard that statement said to me by a church leader. And every time, I wish I had a tape recorder that I could rewind and play back for them so they could hear their own statement. I've found that many times in life we could troubleshoot our situation if we simply listened to ourselves talk about the issue out loud. Try recording yourself talking about it, and then go back and listen with a new perspective. This is why it's important for teams to talk through issues together. What one leader may be blinded to see, another will be able to clearly identify how to fix the dilemma, simply by hearing the teammate state the facts. But, I digress.

Instead, in those moments where I so badly wish that I could play back their firm stance of "we don't do slow songs because our kids don't know how to respond to them," I help them to see the practical steps they can take in order to solve that issue.

Fact: **You don't do slow songs.**

Fact: **Your kids don't understand how to respond to a slow worship song.**

Path to problem solving this issue:

The leader may be unintentionally robbing the kids of having that experience.

Path to problem solving this issue:

If you continue to avoid slower songs, then how will they ever be able to learn?

Path to problem solving this issue:

How will they grow if they never get to experience a slow worship song?

Practical next steps:

Give them the opportunity. Start with one slow song. You may only have space for one each week. You may be limited by time and only be able to do it a couple times a month, but start somewhere. You will not gain any ground in this area until you start. You might stick with the same song repeatedly so they can really learn it. Try not to complicate the experience by teaching them four different slow songs in a month.

If this is really foreign territory to your group, then the beginning point may look like encouraging them to just be still. Allow them to sit or kneel and intently listen to the words. Encourage them to pray before it begins. Maybe you even lead them in a prayer to ask God to speak to them. Pray that God would reveal His nature, who He is, to them during this song. Psalm 46:10 says, "Be still, and know that I am God." Show them how to *know*. Afterward, you could even allow a few kids to share what they heard God speak to them during the song.

This may seem like a baby step, but any crop that yields fruit goes through a process and requires time and attention to be tilled, nurtured, and watered for growth. Just as a farmer doesn't enjoy the plant the day after he plants the seed, this process may take time, but the waiting and hard work will be worth it.

Remember, kids naturally get it. It's within their beings to worship. I've found in the scenarios where kids haven't been given the opportunity to engage in worship that they really just need deeper understanding. I call it "drawing a box." I draw an imaginary box for them around worship. Through teaching little by little, week by week, service by service, I give them knowledge for that box of:

What it encompasses.

Why it's important.

Where they can take part in it.

When their worship matters.

How they can worship.

I can see change in a relatively short amount of time simply because I started changing what I was planting in them.

Just as it says in Hosea 4:6, "My people are destroyed from lack of knowledge," we have a generation of Christians being destroyed from a lack of worship, which is being encouraged by our lack of attention to place importance on and provide knowledge about worship. Both in our churches and in the everyday lives of believers. I understand that may sound harsh. However, if we aren't discipling those we lead to live out the qualities of God's Word, then we are not helping them grow into who they were created to be.

When I lead worship for a group during a week-long VBS or camp, I generally have the kids anywhere from four to eight sessions. The progression through the week is something beautiful. That first day is generally pretty rough, though. In the case of a camp, many different churches and various backgrounds are showing up in the same room. In that first session, I become fully aware of where a certain group is at in their knowledge of worship. I've had cases where I led them in a song and, when I was done, everyone clapped for me as if I had just sung a special of "My Heart Will Go On." (Remember that Celine Dion song from *Titanic*? That was her vocal demo that became the final vocal. How amazing! What a talent. Alright, back to my point.) Watching how the kids respond to my attempt to lead them in worship, I'm able to quickly assess what likely takes place in their weekly church services in the area of worship. In some scenarios, there are kids who get it. But in many situations, I realize I have my work cut out for me. At this moment, I begin to walk out what I shared with you earlier. I start drawing a box around the idea of worship. What is it? Why do we do it? Why is it important? How do they take part in it? Song by song. Set by set. Session by session. I give them understanding, knowledge, and practical how-to's. We make progress. We start taking steps forward.

I will actually encourage them to take a necessary step. Make a choice not to leave the same way you came in. Maybe you have never sung along during worship time. So, the next step for you is to sing along. For some, the next step is to stop being a distraction to others around them. For others, that step may look like closing their eyes to focus on God and simply rest in His presence. Many may take that first step of lifting up their hands to the Lord. I share with them that lifting our hands in worship is a way of showing surrender. It's a way of saying, "I'm all in. I give You all that I am." Just as a young child lifts his or her hands to show their parent that they want to be picked up, the same can be true of us with our Heavenly Father. Taking a step to draw close to God can look like holding our hands up and signaling, "God, hold me, help me. I need You." Even as an adult, it is good to be a child of God. Selah.

I'm always moved by seeing the progression, and let's call it what it is...GROWTH, that happens that week. The last day or two is so sweet and precious as you see kids pursuing the heart of their Father. Blessing Him with the joyful sound that their voices make as they sing, shout, clap, jump, dance and raise outstretched arms to show honor to the Lord. It's a beautiful thing. I know those kids will go home differently than when they arrived. They have experienced a path to run to the Father. I pray that it enables those churches to continue in leading kids with intentionality and purpose, not just checking off boxes on a planning sheet.

Every week, give a nugget of information. It doesn't have to be a three-point sermonette. It just has to be knowledge of the **what, why, where, when and how** of worship. Share something before the first song of **WHY** it's important that we worship. Transition between songs by sharing a practical **HOW** we worship. Make space in your service so they can learn about **WHEN** their worship matters. I'm fully convinced that David worshiped God not just when everything was perfect in his life, but when He needed God to move, show up, and bring a miracle to pass in his life. When you're in the middle of a hard season, even a battle, that is not the time to retreat but to proceed in faith with your song of worship, declaring victory belongs to our God. Teach kids **WHERE** they can take part in worship: Any place and at any time. Worship isn't just a church thing. It's an everyday thing. They can worship God at home. All alone or with their family. They can worship God in their backyard, on their bicycle, on the playground, and with their friends. They can worship God loudly, but also quietly. Almost silent and under their breath. Whether they be at school, out and about running errands, or even at the store. The important thing is to teach them to diligently pursue their King. He loves the sound of their voices. They don't have to sound like a pop star or have the personality of their favorite YouTuber. God just wants their hearts.

He wants who they are. That is **WHAT** worship is. Our response to who God is. The Bible says in Psalm 100, "Make a joyful noise unto the Lord." (KJV) It doesn't say to "make a pitch perfect sound to the Lord." It doesn't say, "make an American Idol or The Voice sound unto the Lord." It says a *joyful* sound. Each of us, as children of God, can choose and find our joy in giving Him the worship and praise that He deserves forevermore.

Every birthday card or letter I received at summer camp would be signed by my mom in the exact same way: "Love God, hate sin." My dad would also say various phrases and have me respond by committing not to partake in a certain behavior or activity. Over the years, that repetition yielded different responses. There were certainly the "there it is again" moments, and maybe even a few eye rolls at times. But, I also remember being awakened in my teen years to those statements and sincerely taking ownership of the character they reflected. Drawing a line to say: I want to honor God with my life. If either of my parents had only shared those things once, or even a few times, I wouldn't have caught on. If you only brush your teeth a few times, then it's unlikely you'd get a good report when you go to the dentist. Anything worth having requires diligence. It requires repetition, over and over again. God's Word is alive and it's active. Yet, the Bible still tells us in Romans 10:17: "So then faith *comes* by hearing, and hearing by the word of God." Our kids, and, for that matter, our congregations, need to hear over and over and over again what worship is and how they take part in it. If we don't lead the way and show them, then who will?

Chapter Sixteen

Candy,
Ice Cream and Lies
We Believe

Kids worship shouldn't be all candy and ice cream. We know the importance of telling our kids that if they eat too much candy they'll get a stomach ache, right? Growing up, I vividly remember one occasion when we had a babysitter while my parents attended a church function. Some family friends of ours brought their kids over that evening, too. At the time, our mall had a big candy store named Mr. Bulky's. It was the kind of place where you could fill the bag yourself. They weigh it and then you pay for the amount of candy you got. I poured a bulk bag full of cotton candy flavored jelly beans. I ate quite a few throughout the evening. In the moment, it felt so good. Let's just say, though, the next day I was not well. My stomach was sick. My body became weak as it flushed the sugar-filled, chemical-laced, pink jelly beans out of my system.

There are days when I look at the landscape of kids worship offerings and hear the conversations other leaders have when they describe what they *think* they need to make kids worship a success that I think about those cotton candy jelly beans.

Responsible parents would never allow their children to only eat a diet of candy and ice cream. In this modern age, we have organic-loving parents who try to eliminate any of the high-fructose sugars, dyes, and chemicals from their food. All good parents know that their kids can't actually live off of pizza or mac n' cheese. There has to be a balance of nutrition that their kids experience. Vegetables, fruits, grains, nuts (aside from allergies, of course) and meat. You can't leave out that protein. Our bodies need those things. We are all aware, both as individuals and as caring parents, that a balanced diet is imperative if you want to live a long, healthy life.

We are spiritual parents to the kids in our ministry. Too often, I see kid's ministry zero in and focus on the wrong things when it comes to kids worship. Have you ever been so close to something that you couldn't see it? The picture is blurry and your eyes can't focus in order to make out the image or read the words on the page. You have to back up, create some space, and only then can your eyes adjust to see clearly. Too many of our churches are feeding kids a diet of only candy and ice cream when it comes to the worship time. I love both, but I know that I need the kale salad, too. I must have the Brussel sprouts and the raspberries. I benefit from the fish and oh how I love the steak! We know that the candy and ice cream aren't lethal when they're experienced in small doses. We all love to have a good treat from time to time, or maybe even daily, if we're honest.

So, hear me when I say, I am not hating on motions in kids worship. In case you haven't quite figured it out, I'm equating non-stop motions to a diet of candy and ice cream. What I *am* doing is hating on that being the ONLY thing you are presenting to your kids. I am disgusted when they're present from start to finish of every song, or when they don't make any sense. Or, when you need to study for six weeks if you're ever going to catch on and be able to do the motions. I speak with so many leaders who have older kids that unplug from the worship time. They roll their eyes, cross their arms, and have basically decided they don't like it. The leaders are often aware that kids are disconnected, but they haven't actually paused long enough to connect the dots between what they are presenting and force-feeding to these kids, and what they actually need. They haven't questioned what they are doing that may be contributing to the push back. Meanwhile, these kids are getting closer to the age when they will determine they "don't want to go to youth group or church anymore." And somehow, their parents will allow that decision. My heart breaks because I realize it could all be done differently. We don't have to push those kids away. We can do better. I have a dream of a better, more well-balanced meal that we consume during our kids worship experiences.

My dad, Jim Wideman, wrote an article for *Kidzmatter* magazine where they highlighted this quote: *"It bothers me that sometimes we have reduced praise and worship for kids to an aerobic exercise rather than an expression of the heart."* I couldn't agree more.

I do believe motions can enhance songs. I also believe that motions can help kids learn and better remember the words to the song. I believe some actions for younger kids can be such a win. It is satisfying when you see the whole room moving in motion, participating in a song. I will share some qualities of what makes great motions, as well as some other tips in creating them, shortly.

But first, I have to speak to the elephant in the room. Too often, Kidmin leaders look around the room during VBS, when the whole place is jumping and spinning to the right two times, and they think, "Yes! We are winning at kids worship! This is the good stuff." But the farther away in the year that you get from VBS, it becomes harder and harder to see that same sort of participation. Maybe the kids are tired of the song. Maybe they are getting older and are less into those actions. Maybe they need a little less candy and a little more fruit, or even some green beans. As leaders, we've sold ourselves short on making worship a win, while we've given ourselves a false sense of participation in worship just because we see everyone doing the motions.

I can't tell you how many times I've seen a post in a group or been speaking face to face with a children's pastor when they tell me, "If the song doesn't have motions, I can't do it." I'm sorry, what? I don't find that commandment in my Bible. I don't remember David singing about that in the Psalms. There are some great songs that need to be sung out there. Many can benefit from motions. But, some do not need motions. It may not be right for that particular song. Plus, if you work with preteens, this is another area you have to think through as you navigate how you are meeting their needs AND preparing them for what's to come in your student ministry.

Over the years, a vicious cycle has been created where products and resources are created to meet needs, but also expectations of what will be included. The local church Kidmin leader requests or demands (depending on how you look at it...wink, wink) motions be included for every song. Publishers and companies start feeding the animal and, over the years, it snowballs into a bit of the monster that we're now dealing with. I wrote music for a VBS curriculum for a number of years. I can tell you firsthand that the motions were included not because they were right for the song or even the best way to lead that song. They were included because they were expected to be there. Some leaders would not be willing to use that VBS curriculum if it didn't include motions for every song from start to finish. Watch me insert my face into the palm of my hands and start crying. The publisher provides the motions because if they don't, you won't buy the product. And over time, instead of leading kids and modeling to worship leaders the *best way* to lead the song, we take part in this circle that goes round and round and round.

Do you hear how absurd all of this is now that you're reading it on paper?

It's time to make the merry-go-round stop.

The motions in a video do not lead the song for you.

They may guarantee a high percentage of participation with action, but no real understanding of why we worship. And that does not equate to effectively discipling kids in worship. It makes me think of the clanging cymbal description of 1 Corinthians 13:1. Could it be that we have a bunch of clanging cymbals in our ministries? Worship in sound, but not in heart. Worship on the planning sheet, but not in genuine participation and sacrifices of praise.

Videos are not bad. They are a tool.

Motions are not bad. They are a tool.

Great songs are not bad. They are a tool.

And all three things are very good. In fact, you need all of those things. Still, if you have all of the right tools but lack a vision for worship, then you're never going to arrive where you need to go. It's like having your family all packed up in the family car, excited and ready for a vacation away. The only issue is you have no idea where you're going. Or, it might mean that you get on the highway headed in the wrong direction. You may have gas in the car. You may have clean clothes and a toothbrush in the suitcase, but without steering the car down the right path for your destination, you won't experience the fun you had planned for your weekend away.

I understand you have too much on your plate. If your to-do list is anything like mine, then there are always more projects to complete then there is time, space, and finances to make them happen. I get that the easier way looks more appealing. You know when you're at the grocery store trying to determine which checkout line will be the fastest one, BUT it didn't work out how you planned? Instead, the line you didn't choose has moved through two other customers in the time you're still waiting to check out. You're stuck and all you can do at this point is shrug your shoulders and just let it be. This may be an area of ministry that's been sitting on the back burner for too long. You may have been relying on motions that make the room move, and you've even convinced yourself that you're developing worshipers. Well, enough is enough. It's time to turn your attention to this area. The time is now to dream about what the next steps are to lead your kids from A to B and then C to D, and on and on. Week by week. Song by song. Teaching moment by teaching moment. Psalm by Psalm. Let's stop cheating our kids out of knowledge and understanding. Let's teach them what worship truly is and how to engage in it.

Again, I'm not hating on motions. I provide motion tutorials to my music. There are whole songs and parts of songs where it makes a ton of sense. However, do you know what I do not do? I don't put motions in my videos. I'll pull the curtain back and tell you why. I am intentional about everything I do. When I put a person doing a specific activity in the song, then that dictates that everyone must do the motion in order to use the song. Rather than a one size fits all worship, why don't we think more in couture fashion terms where measurements are fitted to the person who is going to wear that garment. Ya'll, that will preach! Get your hanky out and wave it now. Post a quote on social media with #sweetsoundbook.

I have enough experience to know that not every church has the same needs. Not everyone has the same wants. You may desire to teach your kids more than one way to participate in worship, which is beautiful and admirable. There are many different types

144

of environments out there. There are many types of programs and services that can benefit from a great song. But here's the thing, more than a singer or doer of songs, I believe you are a worship leader. YOU should determine when the motions make sense. When they will add to and enhance what you're doing and, likewise, when they aren't right.

When I began taking over our elementary worship at my church, Hillsong Kids was releasing a number of albums and kids worship videos. No doubt, they had many great songs. They choreographed everything and had motions, and all of that was great. But, there were times I took half of their motions and I tweaked the other half because it just made more sense for my group. Was I grateful for the resource? Absolutely! I love David & Beci Wakerley so much. They wrote many of those songs and are true pioneers and vision casters for what could be in the area of kids worship. I consider them friends. We have kindred spirits. No offense to what they did and provided, but they were in another country. I was the one in my church who knew my kids and what would work best for each age group. I was the leader who had a vision and a plan for that week's worship set and how each song would work together. I was the one determining how to lead my kids best.

Every church has a DNA and a personality. I've experienced songs that were working everywhere else, (or so it seemed) flop in my congregation, and then other, more obscure, songs in culture be the perfect war cry of praise for us. Don't fall victim to culture peer pressure. Not every song is tailored for your group. Through trial, error, and time you will begin to learn what will resonate and work best with those you lead.

I was consulting with a church in Florida and helping them with their kids worship. I started by watching their Sunday morning service.

They had a ton of kids on stage helping to lead the worship time. They didn't really have a singular worship leader, but that's a different issue for another day. As I watched that morning, I wrote in my notebook, "Are you raising dancers or singers?" There was plenty of movement happening on stage and off. It was exciting. It looked good when you stood in the back corner and saw the action. You probably would've equated it with success. However, the problem was that practically no one was singing the words to the song. (And I'm specifically talking about the kids on stage.) **I have had days where I felt like kid's leaders worshiped the motions more than they were focused on worshiping their Savior.**

When I think about discipling kids to be the worshipers they were made to be, I'm not very focused on the choreography to the song. It's a heart game for me. I want to guide their hearts to be like David. I want them to be so confident that they can call out to God with a song and He will be in their midst. I want to help them learn to run to the Father. Those motions aren't going to get them through when they're 16 years old and tempted by peer pressure. They definitely won't help when the child becomes a 40-year-old adult who is navigating a valley where their spouse walked out on their marriage.

Is there a time and place for motions? Absolutely.

Are motions good? Yes, they can be.

Are all motions needed? No, not really.

I'm in this for the long haul. The reward comes over the span of decades to come. I care about the seeds I'm planting. I want this Sunday to be great. You can absolutely believe I want it to be a success. I am going to cleverly and creatively use the tools that I have learned over the years in leading all ages in worship to connect with my audience and lead them on an age appropriate level. But in doing so, I'm going to serve more than one kind of food and will use more than one ingredient to season the variety of food. Because, candy and ice cream won't sustain you long-term.

I Like To
Move It,
Move It

Now that we've talked about the importance of not overdoing motions, let's talk about how to utilize them wisely and create them effectively.

When I'm looking to create motions to songs the first question I ask is, "What is the obvious motion that comes to mind when you listen to the song?" The obvious motion to me is always the right choice. I love when I travel and I'm singing one of my songs that didn't include a motion tutorial, and yet, when we are singing the words, the kids at the church, as well as myself, end up doing the same movement. To me, that is a fantastic sign that it is the *right* motion. What is the thing that you are compelled to do when you sing that lyric or hear that music? Get in a room with a couple other people and see what your natural reaction to hearing the song is.

I always gravitate toward simple, generic movements more than dance choreography. I think they are much more approachable for a varied group of kids. Jumping is great. Movement of arms and legs. Spinning in a circle. A fist pump. An arm waving back and forth. Simple, easy, movements.

You want the motions to ENHANCE the song, not take away

from it. **If you're too distracted by the motions to try to sing, then your motions are not serving the song well.**

Don't worry about having a motion for the entire song from the first note to the last. I like to say it using this old adage: "Absence makes the heart grow fonder." There are some songs that can really benefit from a motion on the chorus, but then nothing feels right or seems to enhance the verse. So just stand, clap, be energetic on the verse, and then do the motion on the chorus. The scenario could be reversed. I have one song where I just do a fist pump on the chorus and then wave my arms back and forth on the bridge. It works. It isn't too much. And even those who might lean toward being too cool for school are willing to do it because it's just a small amount. But to me, it's still purposeful in engaging those I'm leading.

Remember to have fun! We forget this ingredient too often. Fun is different than silly. I'm not a silly person, but I am a happy and fun person. Silly and fun have different connotations. Silly isn't a very good ingredient to worship the Lamb that was slain for us. However, fun works great as we rally our kids to celebrate the goodness of God. God will not be mocked. Let that be said of our worship, as well.

Next, ask yourself: **"Is that motion something a ten-year-old boy would be willing to do?"**

I will often hear from another leader that the girls love it. That may very well be the case. It's very possible due to the style of your motions or choreography that only the girls are interested in doing that action. Face the facts. There are certain things that a cool boy is not going to be willing to do. You have to consider that. Make sure you are looking at all the facts and decide what is being sacrificed. Is that a sacrifice worth making, or is there something you could tweak or change that may impact the percentage of both your boys and your girls participating?

Find ways for them to participate with you on stage to select songs. I have some props I use for specific songs. Whether it be a superhero cape, racing flag, seasonal hats, stop & go signs, or guitar hero guitars. A great way to engage your whole group is by choosing a couple kids to come up, rock out, and have some fun while reinforcing the message the song is about.

Motions should be a form of action that assists what you're singing, with the goal of engaging those you are leading. It should be something fun that enhances and strengthens the message you are singing about, not take away from it. Song motions should not look like you are miming the song. This is not a game of charades. You are not acting it out. You are using words to communicate as you sing the lyrics. Because some words can be communicated with an action, it is simply another way of engaging the senses and using the sticking power of music to help young hearts soak up the message and truth you're proclaiming in song.

I have mentioned a balanced diet in kids worship, so let me unpack that a bit more. Motions on select songs are good. Also, teaching them to only stand, clap, sing, or participate, whether it be on specific sections or whole songs, is another method. Teaching them the importance of why we lift our hands and giving them the opportunity to do that on slower songs is yet another. It's the Hebrew word YADAH. Inviting them to kneel is a form of worship. It's the Hebrew word BARAK. We unpack those and other Hebrew words for praise in my *Heartbeat* curriculum. It's the number one piece of feedback I receive from leaders, saying their kids loved it and showed up, ready to learn more in the corresponding weeks that followed. They really are hungry and eager to learn about how to participate in worship.

You also need to consider the age range of your group, as well as the next class they will be going into, and what that looks like for your worship time. Have you ever thought about what happens if your kids ministry does non-stop motions and the next class that child goes into is your student ministry, which does not do motions? Insert the "dun, dun, dun" sound effect. What if you sing the same popular worship song but that child has only ever experienced participating in worship with actions? I think that makes for a very awkward, and possibly embarrassing, first day in the youth group. Of course, they're going to stop participating after that tragic experience. Give your kids more than one definition of worship. Start preparing them now for what they will experience in the months ahead. This applies from kindergarten to elementary as well. **Always help them be prepared for what's to come.** This really is a pro-tip that must be a concern for every leader as they lead their area of ministry. **You're meeting the needs of where they are at currently AND you're helping them prepare to grow and develop in the spiritual, just as they are in the physical.**

Stop defining worship as a "one size fits all" style of participation. One of the things I always loved at the Kidjam summer camp by Orange, as well as on the Hillsong Kids videos, is that they had people on stage doing motions. But, they also had worship leaders on stage *not* doing motions. They might have done some select movements, but they also just jammed to the music, stood, clapped, and worshiped. This is a great idea. Show and model more than one way to participate. Not everyone will want to do the motion. Not everyone is content to only clap. Both are good, so do both. By changing what your ask is, you will engage a bigger percentage overall because you're not reducing the participation of worship down to one single thing.

Let me share another story with you that played a big part in how

I processed these feelings and convictions. Years ago, there was a song I did that had some simple motions on the chorus. I would lead the song with a group strictly comprised of preteens and they would do the motions. All was well. Then another Sunday, I'd be in a combined age group elementary class. I'd do the same song with the same motions and guess who wouldn't do those motions? The preteens (aka: oldest kids in the class). Now, at first you might be able to chalk this up to that particular city or group, but I kept repeating the scenario city after city, coast to coast. Same song + same motions + different groups of kids = same results. So these experiences caused me to start asking more direct questions. Why are the preteens willing to do the motions when they are the only ones in the room? But, why won't they do them when the first grader is present? Hmmm. I've had leaders tell me their preteens love motions, and that may be the case. But to me, this reminds me of the parable of the lost sheep, only it's more sheep than just the one. If the motions aren't acceptable to do when the first grader is there, then why would I still have a classroom of fifth graders only worshiping in that way?

I have a very strong conviction through the songs I write, and the music and videos I create, to ensure they send one message: **Jesus is relevant to your life TODAY.** Hebrews 13:8 tells us that "Jesus Christ is the same yesterday and today and forever." Yet, in our ministries, when we force them to do something that doesn't appeal to their likes or potentially embarrasses them, I feel we send a message that Jesus is lame and church isn't cool. I am not willing to project that feeling. I do not want my name attached to that. I am passionate about wanting them to know that Jesus is relevant to their life today...right now. Because He is. It's in this season where they will build that foundation of truth. I want the foundation to be solid before a few years from now, where they may ponder if Jesus still applies to their life. We know that He does, but we have to show them that is true. And it starts with us and the picture of Jesus that we radiate.

What you're pumping through your sound system and projecting on your screens matters. We need to meet the needs of those who we are working so hard to reach. A captain doesn't invite passengers on a boat, make sure they have life jackets, and then push them away from shore while saying, "Good luck!" That captain ensures they get on the ship and then he grabs the wheel. He has a course planned. He watches the gauges. He's aware of the wind and the tide. He navigates all the factors with attention to detail in order to ensure his passengers get where they need to go. This is your purpose.

I will end with this disclaimer: Pray and talk to God about it. Ask Him what you need to do for *your* kids. That's what I did. I'm not at your church, but you are. God knows everything about your group of kids, and you know what? He knows exactly what *you* need to do to best reach those kids. I can only share from my experience and what I have navigated through over the years. And one thing I have learned is that kids change. One generation has needs that are different from another. Most of all, keep fighting for their hearts. Keep pointing them to Jesus. Whatever is the best way for you to focus on those two things, I will champion and support you in. Prayer changes everything. I know God will speak to you, if you'll just ask, listen, and then commit to being obedient to whatever He says.

Chapter Eighteen

God Will Not Be Mocked

One of the most important things we can teach our kids is not to mock worship. It is one thing to not participate respectfully. That is a choice and I realize everyone is in a different place on their journey and walk with God. But, one thing I will never allow is for kids (or leaders) to make fun of what we are doing. That is disrespectful. That is spitting in Jesus' face as far as I'm concerned.

If worship is for Jesus and there's someone making fun of the fact that people are giving a gift of worship to Jesus, that is never acceptable. If you went to a birthday party and another attendee laughed and made fun of the gift you brought, you would probably be offended and think it was rude. If we know that is socially unacceptable behavior at a birthday party, then why in the world are we allowing it in our church classrooms?

Ideally, you have your adult leader volunteers trained on your vision for worship and how to model, lead, and steward responses of worship. But, from time to time you will have someone act out. Maybe they mock someone else's participation. At times, they may attempt to mock something the leader said or did, in a joking way. These things are not okay. When you have your team trained and aware they can easily step in and correct this. "Not right now, Johnny." 'Suzy, that's not how we worship God." A gentle comment. A hand on a shoulder. A reminder and invitation by simply saying, "let's participate and worship God together." Eye contact. A "not this, but instead this" piece of instruction. In most cases, these things will do the trick.

Sadly, I've been on stage a few times where no adult attempted to stop a situation that was exploding like lava from a volcano, coming to conquer the whole village with it's hot lava power. You think I'm being dramatic, but these are the thoughts of the person on stage who is leading a time that's supposed to be about showing honor and giving worship to the Lord. At times, it has felt like one against a thousand. So yes, it's a true confession of how I have felt left out to dry when the other "adults" in the room chose not to step in to help such situations, while I was alone on stage. The one kid doing the mocking gets the attention of the other kids around. That kid is now a leader, but the only issue is, it's a result of wrong behavior. The contagious behavior now has a gang and the posse is growing in size. Alarm, alarm. I'm on stage seeing it all go down and completely distracted by it (kind of like the kids around them), praying and hoping another adult will step in and help. In some of these cases, however, they don't come to the rescue, which means behavior is headed down the drain and I have a complete mess on my hands OR I am the one to do something that will lead the change. In this case, there are a few things I will choose to do.

1. Make eye contact with them. Ohhhh, the power of eye contact. When you lock eyes with someone who knows that he or she is in the wrong, it's amazing how your gaze can convict and communicate that change is needed. This is my first step.

2. At times, step one doesn't work and I have to add a "no" shake of my head. Non-verbally communicating it's not the time for that.

3. It may still require that I have to pause between

songs and have a teaching moment. We are all better for teaching moments we have had in life. Whether from a parent, teacher, coach, or pastor. Teaching moments help guide us down the right path. I can address the whole crowd, pointing out what's wrong, disrespectful, or even the opposite posture we should have during worship. All while teaching them an alternative display that is the good and correct way, with the attitude we should have, and why our heart expression matters. I can teach the whole group while speaking to an issue of a smaller group within.

4. Depending on the degree of mockery or, dare I say, rebellion that is happening, it could mean that we pull aside the person (or persons) afterward. I have found, sometimes, that it's just a hurting kid in need, acting out to be seen. They aren't truly desiring to distract others from worshiping Jesus; there's something else going on in their life. By pulling them aside and talking it through with them, not only can I correct their behavior, but I am able to minister to what's actually hurting and troubling them.

I believe you should have rules and expectations of appropriate behavior. Just as there are manners and social standards for how we interact with each other, there should be space for equivalent things in the church house. By laying these out and having your team aware and on board, everyone better understands how to handle these types of hiccups along the way.

One of the ways to teach and prep for these is by problem solving and analyzing past issues. When "X" happened before, what could have been done to prevent it, stop it, or change it? Talking through past issues and mistakes with your team and worship leaders is always an exercise in problem solving and preparing for how to resolve situations that arise during future times of worship.

Shortly before I started the process of writing this book, I encountered a couple of kid's services where volunteers ran around trying to cheer on the crowd. I was standing off to the side watching it happen. Because of how they encouraged this rally cry with a run around the room, I couldn't help but feel concerned for what they were actually encouraging. I know the volunteer meant well. Unfortunately, I don't think they had considered what their approach was or the behavior it would ultimately lead to. It felt like a bigger distraction than help. Did they really want the kids to randomly mimic their run across the front? Or their untimely cheer when the person leading wasn't asking for that to take place. Remember, silliness is not appropriate for worship time. I repeat: Not appropriate. If you question that, then go look up the definition of the word silly.

These leaders would have been more effective walking up to the one, giving a little nudge or making eye contact, and giving a personal invitation to join in to the time of worship. Make sure your efforts are helping and not hurting the situation. Always add to and support those who have the authority to lead the time. If what you're doing is taking away from their authority, or it's encouraging something different to happen that could be considered a mockery of the moment, then please refrain from doing it.

I believe that worship is our response to who God is and what

He has done and is doing in our lives. Does the response you're getting during worship times reflect honor and awe? Or rather, an attitude or spirit of selfishness?

Do you allow sitting? I think there can be a time and place for it. I mentioned that when beginning the process of teaching kids how to engage with a slow worship song, and even with preschool kids, by inviting them to sit. It very well could be the answer. There could be times during a post-message response song or worship time that allowing them to sit as they pray, kneel, or respond to the message may be the best, and appropriate, choice. Still, as you make it farther down the path of worship, a sitter is like the opposite outcome of popcorn popping. It's the one retracting which can have the dramatic effect of dominos and before you know it, the one turned into ten, turned into the whole section. You now lost control and it's all because one child sat down. There can be exceptions to everything. I understand that they can have a physical reason for it. But even still, this is where your team acts as support to your worship leader, team, and band on stage. The one leader walks over to find out if they are alright. Why did they sit? Are they checking out? Did they quit? Do they need prayer? There are many reasons for why it could have been, but this is why it's so important to have your team check into what's happening. It's crucial to remind the group what the time is about and why we stand. Let them know that we are first and foremost showing honor to God with this time. Consider how you can bring them back in and remind them of how to engage. As a worship leader, my heart is always to engage and draw them back into what we're doing rather than allow them to lead others down the same path.

In so many cases, kids need you to draw a box around what worship is and what it's about. This happens early on when you're beginning the process of teaching them about worship. But, it is also needed in different seasons. Transitions and shifts throughout the year where kids moved on and other kids moved up. A new room and different teachers may require a refresher in what worship time is about and how we do it. This is an ongoing process as your church continues to grow. I'm not saying to box worship in. I am saying to draw a box around the idea of worship and show basic ways to engage with it for those who need a deeper understanding. Why does this time even matter? Think of it as a protected area for them to learn and grow in. Have you ever ridden bumper cars? I've only ever seen bumper cars within a protected corral or course. I've never seen bumper cars on the loose, having a free-for-all down the street. That's for a different experience, like a 4-wheeler in an open field or a golf cart in a neighborhood. On a bumper car ride you are kept within a certain area, guided by the bumpers. And you're safe while you do it.

It's not enough to teach them what to worship. As worship leaders, you've got to teach them *how* to worship.

Here are some things to think about, define, and train your team to lead through:

- What are some examples of mockery behavior you've experienced in the past?
- What are some types of behavior you want to discourage?
- What types of engagement and participation do you want to welcome?
- How do you want your leaders to gently correct and lead the kids through encouragement?

Encourage your worship leaders to build relationships with the kids. I cannot stress this enough. The ones who they get to know and talk to before class will become some of the first to enter in when it's time to worship. It's amazing how relationship can make a huge difference. If you do activities or have special events throughout the year, invite your worship team to help you at those events. Playing putt-putt or managing an activity at a game-night will pay off big Sunday morning at 9am. Small talk about when their birthday is, what they like to do for fun, or a sport they play can be the difference maker in that child feeling seen or invisible. Even in the areas where we had a band leading worship, I would remind them that not every person is going to relate and connect with me. Some would be drawn to the guy playing drums. Others to the person playing bass. TOGETHER we are able to reach so many more than we ever could on our own. Their presence makes a difference. Encourage them to take responsibility for leading the kids. Their actions on stage, and especially the ones off stage, are the necessary ingredients that have the power to impact a generation.

At the end of the day, it's all about helping those we are leading in worship take a step. One step is all that I ask and challenge them to take each time we gather. But if they show up 30 times this next year, and they take a step in their worship every time, then my oh my, look at how much growth you will have in that one life. Repeat that in every regular attendee. Repeat that in those you only see a few times a year. Give that challenge to those who attend your VBS or go to summer camp. Before you know it, just like wildfire, the flame you lit is being fanned and the fire within their spirit is getting bigger as it grows.

Chapter Nineteen

Made to Praise: Preschool Worship

Every preschool event I've ever been a part of was truly an original. There are no duplicates. No moment is recreated and every moment is a bit unpredictable. I'm sure you know this to be true. You may have multiple services, but every class happens differently than the group before. At my preschool-aged concerts, kids just randomly appear on stage, much to my surprise. It's the nature of this age group. I love the adventure that it is. There is an extra layer of sweetness on these young hearts as they raise up a holy sound to the Lord. They don't sing along to every word, but the words they do sing are so precious. I believe our youngest kids are marked by the truth of God's Word in the music we present to them. I can tell you as a parent that when one of my boys started singing a song throughout the day that they had learned in church, my heart and spirit swelled. I believe families are impacted by the praise of these young ones. May we raise them up to fall in love with time spent in the presence of the King.

Refrain from looking at song time in class as just another thing to do or as a nuisance. Remember there is power in the worship of "nursing infants and toddler shouts," as we have learned from Psalm 8:1-2. Hold that verse near to your heart. In every moment that is difficult or feels like a struggle, realize that you are guiding young warriors to offer up their gift of praise that echoes through Heaven.

I was looking at scripture one day and noticed that children worshiping Jesus plays a part in our salvation story. It's the passage where Jesus was riding on the donkey. The crowds were shouting "Hosanna!" You might recognize this as the Palm Sunday story that we celebrate every year. They were waving the palm branches and crying out, "Hosanna in the highest." But the chief priests and teachers questioned what they were hearing. Maybe your own pastor, staff, and volunteer team have questioned the worship of kids. You're in good company with Jesus. Look at how he replied. Matthew 21:16 says, "Do you hear what these children are saying?" they asked him. "Yes," replied Jesus, "have you never read, "'From the lips of children and infants you, Lord, have called forth your praise'?" Yes, right there Jesus is quoting that verse in Psalm 8:2. I'm waving my hanky right now. Preach it Jesus. I love that we have various versions of the scripture. So often looking at the verse in a different translation helps us better understand the magnitude of what is being said.

The NLT says, "You have **taught** children and infants to give you praise."

The NKJV says, "Out of the mouth of babes you have **perfected** praise."

The ISV says, "You have **created** praise."

The TPT says, "You have **fashioned** the lips of children and little ones to **compose** your praises."

Soak in those words for just a second. **God has taught, perfected, created, and fashioned little ones to compose His praises.** Making time for kids to worship in your classrooms is one of the greatest things you could do with the time you have been entrusted with to lead them.

Sweet Sound

There is a cosmic chorus of praise where preschool kids are identified as being a part of the orchestra sound. Psalm 148:10-13 says, "Praise him, all beasts and birds, mice and men, kings, queens, princes, and princesses, young men and maidens, children and babes, old and young alike, everyone everywhere! Let them all join in with this orchestra of praise. For the name of the Lord is the only name we raise!" (TPT)

We all worship something in our lives. Every human on planet Earth was created to worship. It's innate in us to worship something. Some people worship a car or a job. Others worship social media or video games. Some adore celebrity status or the latest fashion. Those things consume them and their obsessions. In 1 John 5:21, we are instructed that Jesus should be the subject and focus of our praise. It says, "So, little children, guard yourselves from worshiping anything but him." (TPT) I love how the NLT puts it: "Keep away from anything that might take God's place in your hearts." As a leader, I have a responsibility to help others learn and live out the Word of God. I want to lead well in guarding our children from worshiping anything but Jesus and allowing the things of earth to take the place in their hearts that should only belong to Him. This is our why and our marching orders in leading them well.

When you are intentional about creating spaces for kids to sing God's praise, it creates a shift in the atmosphere. The power of God is unlocked and invited to live, move, and have its being in their midst. Do you want to raise world changers for the Kingdom of God? Then make it a point for kids to praise God every time you gather. Put His praises on their lips. Life and death are in the power of the tongue. Help them speak and sing life through choruses of worship!

For preschool children, choosing age-appropriate songs is very important. You have to remember that little ones have short attention spans. Songs for this age group should be 2-3 minutes in length. They should be simple and repetitive songs. There's a couple exceptions to this time qualification that can make a song go outside the lines of this recommendation. The first one is repetition. A song like "Father Abraham" is going to be at least three minutes by the time you do both arms, legs, nod your head, spin in a circle, etc. So, why does this get an exception? The actual song is repetitive. It's one section sung over and over mixed with a different action. You could come up with new action phrases and sing it for six minutes and it would likely work, although everyone would be very, very tired in the end. The other exception is found in the "BPM." What's BPM, you ask? It stands for "beats per minute." Fast songs have a higher BPM number. Slower songs have a slower BPM number. Slower songs are just that s l o w e r, therefore they take more time to happen in life. That's why you may have noticed that most slow ballads are four to five minutes in length, even on the radio, whereas a fast song is only around three. A slower song is going to take a little longer. You're not going to find a two-minute slow song, and that's perfectly alright.

Back in the day when "How Great Is Our God" was a new worship song, I felt like that was a chorus that preschoolers could sing. They didn't need to sing the verses about the "Lion and the Lamb," but I knew they could sing that simple chorus. So, I made an edit of the song. There's music software like Pro Tools and Logic, or every Apple computer that has Garage Band, that are all user-friendly. I went in and chopped up the arrangement and made the chorus repeat a few times, and then a couple times through the bridge. This enabled me to sing that song with our preschool kids. I later recorded a version like this that's available on the first "Little Praise Party: My Best Friend" album. My point, though, is that you may have a song that is starting to become an anthem of your church. There may be one section of the song that you feel would work with your young kids. Find a young person or ask your tech or worship department to help you make an edit that is preschool-sized. I'll never forget a mom stopping me to tell me how moved she was when her son started singing the song at home one day. She thought it was so cool that her two-year-old was singing the same anthems that she was in "big church." That song of worship united this family to sing together in celebration of the greatness of God. What you do goes beyond the four walls of your classroom.

Your youngest 2 and 3 year olds need simplicity in their songs. They also need repetition. I try really hard to repeat some of the same phrases in the songs I write for little ones because I know the more we keep repeating it, the greater the opportunity that those young children will latch on and sing it. It's learning to say what you need to say by using the fewest amount of words, but also repeating those same words as much as possible. With this age group, I also realize they aren't going to sing every word from start to finish. But I have found they will sing some of the words. Their ability to sing along in some portion of the song is the win here. Simplicity and repetition will make those things more achievable.

Repetition increases understanding. The first time something is heard, 10% is retained. The second time it's heard, 25% is retained. The third time 50% and the fourth time 75% is retained. It truly takes repetition for us to get it.

As children are reaching that five-year-old age, you will find that they love call and response type songs. Songs where the leader sings something and they get to repeat it back. It may happen the entire song, like in "Sunday School Rock," or it may happen in one section, like on the bridge of my song, "Shout!" You'll also notice that these older kids are becoming better able to handle multiple parts of a song. For example, a verse and a chorus.

I have some really good news for you. You do not need a huge repertoire of songs. Your preschool ministry doesn't need a songbook of 50 songs. As any parent has ever learned, children love the same thing over and over again. I'm sure you're thinking of a particular movie, show, or book that your child repeatedly requested even though they had experienced it hundreds of times before. Preschool children love routine and familiarity. Unlike the rest of us, they aren't looking for the next new thing. They just want more of what they already have grown to love.

I have known of churches that pick a group of songs and sing the same ones each week for a month. There are others that have some variety each week, but have a key song that fits their theme and lessons for that month, so they will repeat it each week. I don't believe there's a right or wrong way here. My suggestion is to try out a few different methods over the next quarter and see what method works best for both your kids and your teachers. Find what works and do that.

My words of wisdom to you are to be careful not to do too many songs back to back. A 30-minute preschool worship set is not going to go well. They're not going to sing five songs back to back very effectively. It's important to remember attention spans and plan your service accordingly.

Now, you can do a couple songs back to back and that should work great. Maybe even three songs, depending on their type. I share about song sets and desires as a worship leader in chapter 12, but this same concept applies here.

You can lead preschool kids in worship, and do it well. To hear them singing the old chorus "God Is So Good," is oh so sweet. I have found that placing a slower worship song after something that is very high energy and active works really well. I may transition from my arrangement of "Father Abraham," where we are all tired and out of breath, to then have them sit down, inviting them to be still and think about something they have to be thankful to God for. What's one thing that God has done for you that you can be thankful for? I can encourage and ask them to focus on worship a little bit more after they are a bit tired from the big activity song, then if I placed it after they had already been sitting for a lesson time.

To lead the song well, you also have to *know* the song. It is imperative that even your teachers take time during the week to learn and be familiar with the song. Listening to the song as you drive to church on Sunday morning isn't enough. Pushing play on a song is the first step. Knowing the song so you can lead it and coach others to participate in it requires some time and preparation. The difference in the outcome makes the effort totally worth it.

It's always a good idea to do your research. What are some successful shows and music specifically directed toward preschoolers? There are some of you who have young kids at home and this is your current world. For others, it's been a few years since Mr. Rogers. (I mean, let's take a moment to give thanks for him. I went to Pittsburgh and saw the original sets of the show at the Heinz museum. It was like reliving my childhood. I couldn't believe my eyes. Most importantly, I was so moved reading the text about how Fred saw the show as his mission field. There is so much wisdom we can still glean from him). Ask a few parents as they pick up their kids next week what their favorite shows are. What do they listen to in the car? Watch and listen to some of those things. What can you learn from them? How do they communicate? What colors are they filled with? What do you hear in the songs they utilize that may be more approachable than what you've been singing in your classroom? What do you see that you could translate and apply in your classroom setting? There is always something new to learn and I believe we can even be inspired by things created outside of Christian culture, and then use those winning methods for the Kingdom to captivate our children with the love of Jesus.

Language is so important. For our kids to learn, they have to be able to understand the words. Vocabulary is a key ingredient to the songs you sing. The concept of abstract vs. concrete is crucial here. Preschool kids need songs with concrete words. It's hard for them to understand "Jesus is my Savior," but they can comprehend "Jesus is my friend." They might not understand that worship is something we do because "God is holy and worthy of our praise," but they can comprehend that "We sing to Jesus because we love Him." Even at a young age, they understand the concept of love. They love their momma, their grandma, and their favorite teddy bear or special toy. Singing to Jesus because we love Him is an approachable explanation of worship for this age. It's not enough to make sure that your songs are understood, but as a leader, you also need to speak and use words they can understand as you lead them.

Find ways to get them involved, as well. Here are some of my go to's: clap, jump, dance, spin in circles, wiggle, specific motions, hands raised, standing up, sitting down, shouting out, whispering, playing air guitar, etc. I love to have some props on hand, too. Not for every single song, but to make certain songs special and communicate in new ways. I have some plush instruments I have collected over the years. I have foam guitars I bought from a company that was selling puppet supplies. They're the perfect size for young kids, plus they're foam so they can't hurt them or anyone else. I have dress-up props and even a variety of felt hats and crowns. I love to find things that tie into the theme of a song. I have race flags for my "Ready Set Go" song, rubber ducks and bath toys for "The Bath Song," and superhero capes for "Super Wonderful" and "My God Is Number One." Please note: I don't use these for every single song, but rather to enhance a specific song. In some cases, I may have enough props for everyone in class. In others, I choose two to five kids to come up and help me with that song. That day, they are the ones who get the fun items and on another day, there are other kids who will be chosen to help. In church and at school, there's a lot of time and opportunities. It's all about finding new methods to communicate and keep things fresh, exciting, and interesting.

Motions adding physical activity to songs can also be a huge win. I talk about this in depth in chapter 17, so reference that for more on this topic.

Wear bright colors. All black worked great for Johnny Cash. It's slimming, I get it. But all black isn't very cheery and happy. When you watch preschool shows, you'll notice lots of bright colors. It is automatically happier. Wearing bright colors and bold patterns makes you more approachable, especially to young kids.

By now you are probably wondering what qualities make a great preschool worship leader. As you look to recruit new people on your team, here are some things to consider.

You are looking for someone who is willing to have **FUN** with the kids. We aren't looking for a grumpy, sourpuss type. We want someone who is willing to jump, wiggle, or cluck like a chicken, if that's what the song calls for. There is certainly an element of laying down your pride in preschool worship. You want someone who is ready to be the leader/conductor of the praise party! We know that the way you communicate can inspire wonder.

PERSONALITY is another characteristic that can make communication more effective. Have you noticed how preschool communicators speak differently and more high-pitched to children than when they speak to adults?

I believe that a **COMMITMENT TO EXCELLENCE** is important, as well. You need leaders who are willing to show up prepared and ready, not looking at the lesson plans for the first time during the class time. Leaders who will be coachable and will welcome evaluation and feedback in order to grow.

Although **MUSIC/SINGING EXPERIENCE** is preferred, it's not required. Chances are your preschool worship time is using a pre-recorded song. Your leaders can rely on those vocals. They just need to know the songs and be both creative and diligent to lead the kids through them. Even still, some great people to consider helping you lead preschool worship would be middle school and high school students. Also musically talented moms who may have laid down their own dreams of music and activities in this season of being mom. They may be itching for an outlet and a place to belong. They just need someone to give them the opportunity. Consider young adult couples, too. Young marrieds are often looking for a way they can serve together. This may be the teamwork they are seeking. Folks with backgrounds in drama and theater can also have the right type of performance charisma you're looking for.

Lastly, a **HEART FOR WORSHIP** is a necessity. They must look at this as more than just music time in class. They may already be passionate about worship, or you may have to lead and coach them to grow in this area. Share this book with them. Give them resources and tools to grow in their understanding of worship so they can then pass that on to the kids they will be able to lead.

I am excited for you to be more intentional as you guide young children to give their worship to their best friend, Jesus. What a gift to be one of the very first to lead and point them to a loving Creator who has a plan and purpose for each of their lives. May they cry, "Hosanna! Hosanna!" all of their days.

Chapter Twenty

Play by the Rules: Pro-tips About Usage, Streaming, and Copyrights

As a leader, it's important to **consider a cost per use analysis of the songs and videos you purchase for ministry.** Most leaders don't bat an eye at how much they spend on snacks, balloons, or even within their online Amazon account. It somehow all seems necessary. However, I've heard leaders balk at the cost of videos or only finding one song they could use on an album. One song that's a perfect addition was a worthy find and even the entire cost of an album. Ask yourself these questions:

How many times will you use the song?
Do you have multiple services?
Do you also have midweek services?
Will you use it at camp or VBS?
Is it also on a pre-service playlist?
How many years will you use it?

Every time that song is used in a service, your cost per use just went down. I once did the math on this with a popular song of mine and realized the churches that had purchased this song early on for their ministry, with normal use and repetition, were only spending pennies per use on the song. That is a win! That is actual, affordable change in order to accomplish ministry more effectively. If you've been guilty of some of these confessions in the past, then I challenge you to get a pencil, paper, and calculator and look at the real numbers. I think your perspective will shift. In fact, you may quickly realize that music is one of the most inexpensive and cost-effective resources you use in ministry.

Do you struggle with your budget for worship and media? There are some really great resources available today. There will be a cost attached to utilize them because there's a cost attached for the team of people who created them. It's like the circle of life. You have to have one in order to have the other. Please respect that. (All the songwriters, music producers, and video creators said, "Amen.") If you want to have great content in the future, then you must support these creators in the current season so they can have a future at creating. In reality, there's no such thing as free. The only one who can give you something is the person who has ownership of the creation. People who have copies they obtained the right way can't give you a copy the wrong way. That is sinful. It's not *just* a song. It's not *just* a video. I hope you realize that behind every song there's a long list of people who worked tirelessly on it. Just as you expect to be paid when you do your job, songwriters, musicians, singers, producers, mix and master engineers, graphic designers, and video creators would all like to receive a paycheck for their work, too.

FREE Resources
I have good news. There are some awesome megachurches who create resources for their ministry and have platforms to pass those

on to other churches to benefit from. They are able to bless a lot of ministries because of their faithful, tithe-paying members. If budget is an issue for you, then access those resources that have been given and made available to you. Currently, a short list of those are Life Church Open, Kids On the Move, and Kidspring. Access these great resources as they are readily available to you. Don't forget to be the one who goes back and says "thank you." Send them a card, email, or note on social media and let them know that what they do has blessed you and impacted the lives of those you work with. I promise your note will make their day. Sadly, so very few come back and say "thank you." I learned that lesson from the ten lepers who Jesus healed. Always be the one who goes back and expresses appreciation.

I would challenge you to try not to become "God" in meeting your needs. If your family was going through hardship, would you go to your local grocery store and steal food from the store to feed your family? When you got caught would you make the excuse that your family was in need, therefore, it was okay for you to steal? Although they would have compassion on your situation, it's unlikely the grocery store chain owner or the police officer would say, "Well then, go right ahead and take what you need." There are rules and laws for a reason.

Would you go to a restaurant featuring a buffet and purchase a dinner for you, but also bring in suitcases to fill up with food? All so you can feed your church at a big event you're having. Can you imagine the looks you would get? It's all you can eat for one, not for your entourage. There's a reason why many buffets have policies of "no to-go boxes." People are not always honest. It's sad, but it's also true. We know it sounds ludicrous to think of feeding a huge group of people off food that was only purchased for one. However, good people, who are Christian leaders, are guilty of breaking these same types of rules when it comes to intellectual property. Intellectual property is defined as an invention of the human intellect that involves creativity, such as a manuscript, software, graphic design, song, or video. The creator has legal rights to it and may apply for a copyright, trademark, patent, etc. After knowing that, "I can play it off of YouTube" means absolutely nothing. When you read the terms of use on their site, it actually says it's not for commercial use. Your family is *not* commercial use. Your church family *is* commercial use. The financial side of YouTube is paying micro pennies based on one or two sets of eyes seeing it. They aren't paying the master owner based on your 10, 100, 500, 1,000 eyes seeing that video. The same is also true of your audio streaming service. Unless you have a business music streaming account (remember, you *are* commercial use), then you need to make sure you have purchased audio files to play in your classroom.

"I pay money for this ripping software that eliminates ads" is not a solution for ministry. It's called stealing. Yep, there's a commandment about that. Exodus 20:15 says, "You shall not steal." YouTube stays in business by selling those ads. By removing them, you are cheating YouTube, the advertisers, and video owners like me. Far too many times, I've seen a church leader telling other church leaders how to steal content. My jaw drops. My heart feels like it was stomped on and someone spit in my face. So, I'm a truth teller. Honesty is always the best policy. The YouTube terms of use do not allow you to download the video or play it for a group. It's bad enough when you play it off the system site. But when you rip it off that network, you actually cut the lifeline of very small residuals (how many zeros do you like to see before a number?) You've extracted the video from the living mechanism it was attached to. Do you take the time to read the description on the video or the channel? Does it say how it can be used or how to access it if you need it for a group, commercial setting? Click where it says "learn more" or "about." Send a message or email when needed. Most importantly, play by the rules. God is watching. And so are your kids. Let's all be a great example of how to live ethical lives.

Did you know that playing a movie in your church requires a license to show it to a group? You can't just take your DVD from home or sign-in to your Netflix account and press play. You know the warning messages and fine print at the beginning and ending of a movie? It again states "for non-commercial usage." There are single view licenses available for specific movies. There are also blanket licenses you can get to cover many things on an annual basis. Do the due diligence needed because it matters.

In the past, I've seen church leaders justify stealing because of their need and lack of budget. (I'm sad on many levels that I just typed that sentence.) I completely understand the need and not always having a budget for what you want. I would imagine very few have the budget dollars for everything they want. For all of my adult life, I have made a living from writing and recording songs. So, if you're thinking this is personal to me, then you are correct. I remember a particular back and forth conversation that took place in a group online. It was between myself, some fellow creators, and Kidmin leaders. As the illegal recommendations were being made and as their "lack" became an excuse as to *why* they steal, the sadder I became as I processed it all. Why? Because this leader was trying to put himself in God's shoes in order to fill the need rather than put his trust in God to meet and provide for the need. Do you see the difference?

I'd sure like to think that I listen to God and hear His voice. There are many occasions where I hear someone's story and I respond to that story because I feel His nudge to. When the Holy Spirit prompts me, you can rest assured that I will give and sow, whether that be financial or through the resources I've been entrusted with. The more I processed this exchange that had happened online, the angrier I became because I realized this person didn't just steal from me, my friends, or even competitors, in the natural. By not sharing his story and by failing to tell us the need he was facing in the ministry and not allowing us the opportunity to hear God speak to us about how to respond, this leader was actually robbing me, in the spiritual realm, of the blessing of my obedience. I know that when I give and sow God will always take care of me and meet the needs of my family and the ministry that I represent. It's a spiritual principle. I would rather *give* resources to you all day long than have you steal them off the internet. I want to lay my head on the pillow at night knowing I was obedient to what God told me to do instead of feeling violated by the very group of people I'm trying to help in the first place. I have a feeling many of my peers would back that statement up. Invite us into your story. Tell us what you're doing. Allow the Holy Spirit to tell us, "Help them," "Go there," "Give them a financial gift." Put your trust in God enough to provide for you. In doing so, you'll also end up with a testimony of how God provided that you can share with your church and your kids. Doesn't that seem like the better way that will bear so much more fruit in the long run?

Making and Sharing Videos Online

Just because you *can* make a video doesn't mean that you can make whatever video you want when you are using elements that are the intellectual property of another. I've seen many churches create a dance video using a pre-recorded song, and, at times, even include someone else's video within their video. Although they can make a video using their own visuals with a song they purchased for their church, they cannot distribute that song and make it available to other churches without licensing the content (audio master and/or video master) they included in the video. If any part of a video includes visuals (videos, pictures, etc) from another video they didn't make, it can't be legally uploaded to YouTube or used in church without getting permission from the owner of the visuals.

Online church has become a wonderful tool and option to reach families. Remember to clear your online usage with your curriculum and resource providers. Every company has different options and policies on how you can use it in your classrooms and in online settings. Ask questions. Call the company. Message them and find out the appropriate guidelines and usage that they offer. As the world shifted and quickly changed at the onset of Covid-19, I worked quickly to make online usage options available for my songs and videos. Learn about it at YancyMinistries.com/streaming. Many others did as well, which means you will likely need additional web license and stream licensing for the audio and video masters. For the songwriter license, Christian Copyright Licensing International, commonly known as CCLI, has an add-on streaming license that covers songs being sung. They've also launched an upgrade to their streaming license with the streaming plus license that allows use of audio masters in online church services. Get the appropriate licensing you need for your church. No excuses.

Campuses and Multi-site Locations

I love that so many churches have replicated themselves in locations across their city and even, at times, across state lines. It's important to realize that, in most cases, every one of those locations will require its own copy of that video, song, or curriculum. Just as that location has its own address and an additional staff member who was hired, each campus needs their own copy. You're not sharing toilets or sound systems. You're buying more goldfish snacks and computers for check-in systems. Just because you can throw a video on your web server and allow multiple campuses to access it, doesn't mean you have the right to do that. It's timely to ask the question, "What would Jesus do?" You may have a couple campuses. You could have 5, 12, or over 30. Each one is a location. Here's a good rule of thumb to remember: if you bought a TV, projector, sound system, or boombox for the room, just like the device you're playing it through, that room needs its own individual copy of the song/video.

These issues I've shared about are like cancers within church leadership. It's yucky. It's sickness. It's not right or fair. It's time to say enough is enough to this disease. Honor those who are creating things that bless your church family and strengthen your ability to do ministry more effectively. Jesus performed miracles but he didn't steal the things he used to perform the miracles with. I believe Jesus can and will do amazing miracles in our lives. He really is that great and powerful. I want to bring Him what I have been entrusted with and offer it up to Him knowing that, in His hands, the miraculous will happen. I don't have to force it. I have to trust and believe. Just like you wouldn't steal from a bank, don't steal from your brothers, sisters, and co-laborers in Christ. I truly believe a lot of it is ignorance. Often leaders don't know about proper usage, or maybe they were given poor advice about piracy. The truth will set you free! I hope you hear my heart on this. Please know I share all of this in grace and love. But now that you've been given the truth, use it for good. Do things the right way. May we walk in integrity and model righteousness to those who we lead. May He be glorified through the work and due diligence of our hands.

What is CCLI?

Reporting your song usage really does make a difference.

CCLI is a gift to the Church and to songwriters. They are an international organization that was born out of meeting a need to make song performance licensing available for church services. It's highly likely that your church already partners with them. You obtain a license annually based on the size of your church attendance. Maybe you've noticed the song lyrics on the screen in your sanctuary and the fine print that has a CCLI# at the bottom. Talk with your worship pastor about this and find out who is responsible for it at your church. Your church periodically reports their song usage and from this data CCLI determines what are the most-played songs. Then, they divide the pie of funds among the songwriters to reward and pay them for all the song lyric impressions and times that song has been viewed, displayed, and sung in our congregations. I believe your children's ministry is just as much a part of your congregation as your senior citizens are. If you don't already, choose to report the songs you sing in your kids' classrooms, too. It won't cost you anything but your time to do it. However, the money your church is already paying will get applied and distributed to those who have actually written the songs that have benefited your church. As a songwriter, I can personally attest that your reporting makes a difference in my life and family. Those bi-annual checks received make a huge difference for us. They enable us to take a vacation, or simply pay our bills each month. Your reporting is life-giving to songwriters and their families. From the bottom of my heart, I thank you for doing it.

CCLI has many additional add-ons you can obtain for rehearsals, streaming, using masters in a stream, and even the ability to show certain movies. Dive in and make sure your church has the appropriate licenses for your usage needs.

Chapter Twenty-one

Empowering Families to Worship

In children's ministry, we have the unique privilege to help families learn what it looks like to worship as a unit. Here are a few of my favorite ways to teach them how to do that:

Building Playlists

One of the best ways that you can support families worshiping together is by providing a playlist to parents. Take the songs that you are actively using in your ministry and build a playlist on Apple Music and Spotify to disciple them in worship Monday through Saturday. You may want to do this update monthly. Quarterly is also a great solution and way to keep things fresh. If you can select a specific group of songs for the year, then an annual playlist suffices. Most importantly, you're placing the songs that you use in your ministry in the hands of families so they can push play in the family minivan or living room. It will be faith-filled truths that our kids need. Parents will get to hear the worship of their kids. Families can unite their voices as one and worship the Lord together. What a win! It's also a great way to introduce new songs you plan to use. Add them to your playlist in the mix of the ones they already know.

Building these types of playlists is a completely legal way to obtain the songs you sing and then get them in the hands of families at zero cost to you. There's no special licensing involved with fees you'll need to pay. There's no bulk CD purchases for you to give the music away. When the parent clicks the link you provide to the playlist, they are able to play the music on their personal account with that music streaming service. (Whether they have a free or a paid account, they are able to access what you provide in the same way.)

When you create playlist links, you can provide them in emails you send, newsletters, slides before service, announcement screens in your lobbies, and even social media posts. You could also create a QR code on a take-home paper from class where the parents can scan it with their phone and the playlist pulls up automatically. There are many ways to get the music in the hands of your parents. The only expense involved is the cost of your time to build it and share it. I think it's a pretty cool method to bring church into the other six days of the week for your kids. Think about the conversations they may have because the song triggered a memory the child had from class. Maybe it was something they learned. It could be a scripture they were taught, or a new friend they made. What a gift to help families interact with their kids and help them grow and form their faith. Music has the power to do that.

There are services you can subscribe to that will build a single smart link that you can then program for various music services. So let's say if you want it available at Apple Music, Spotify, YouTube Music and YouTube video, you can build all of those and then place the links under the umbrella of one smart link. Because technology is always evolving, I'd suggest doing a Google search to help you find the most current options.

Social Media

Utilize your social media throughout the week so families will have the ability to interact with the playlist you built. Remind them to listen to a specific song on the way to/from school that goes along with your lesson from that week. Suggest that they have a family praise party. Crank up the music to "song you suggest" and have a living room praise party. Provide some discussion points about a song to help a parent navigate a conversation with their child about the message you're using in worship.

I've seen churches have a #WorshipWednesday type hashtag and then highlight a different song each week that they are encouraging their families to listen and jam out to. I love the rhythm that creates by being an on-going feature parents can learn to expect and be ready for.

There are many different ways to capitalize on this resource and to disciple your families. Remember, music is a tool we have to help God's Word become stuck in their ears and to grow their spirit man. As a famous webslinger once said, "With great power comes great responsibility."

Provide Events for Families to Gather

I'll never forget the night it all clicked. It was one of those light bulb moments that happens from time to time. I had brought my oldest son to our Performing Arts Center in downtown Nashville to see Paw Patrol Live. I wasn't the only one. Hundreds of families had made the journey. Paid for parking. Possibly walked several blocks to get inside. They bought tickets that weren't inexpensive. They were getting snacks and purchasing flashing light toys from an employee working the aisles. These same parents were buying stuffed animals of the Paw Patrol pups that they probably could have bought from a big box store down the street for half the price. As a parent, I was guilty of many of the things I just named. I looked around the room and realized that parents truly desire to create memories with their kids. In fact, they will go to great lengths, trouble, inconvenience and expense to do something fun with their children. Why do they do it? Because in a couple months, something in a conversation will be said that reminds both parent and child of that night they went downtown together and had that really cool experience. The impact goes beyond just a few months. There are things that happened years ago with my kids and when we see that specific souvenir around the house, we talk about how and where we got it. Every parent wants to fill their child's mind with happy, fun, joyful memories of being together. It's the opposite of parental guilt. When they are all grown you will still have the memories, pictures, and well, some wrinkles, too.

That night, I realized the opportunity that the Church often forfeits to help families create memories together. How many lost opportunities have we missed because we didn't provide an outlet for families to come through our doors beyond Sunday morning? This experience made me even more thankful for the churches I am able to work with that give families a space to create memories together through family worship concerts and Christmas events. How cool that not only can our churches create fun activities and have yummy snacks and souvenirs to take home, but it can also be centered around the Gospel and help grow the faith of generations.

There's an awesome church in Alabama I have worked with many times. We've done a couple of "Waffle & Wiggles" preschool events together. Yep, you guessed it. They serve waffles. We then come together and wiggle and sing with a Little Praise Party concert for these families. They close out the time with some inflatables and fun games for the kids. These events have been a blast, but what stays with me is the look in parents' eyes when they would stop and talk to me. The look they had as they said "thank you" and "I'm so glad we came" was a look of pure delight and pride unlike I've ever seen. This church loved on their families in a way that was worth every penny of expense. Every minute of time invested in promoting and planning reaped a harvest that is still having ripple effects.

My challenge to you is to find a way to serve families gathering together. Imagine if more people had memories centered around the Church and experiencing the abundant life Jesus offers us.

Family Devotional Resources

How can you provide resources for your families to grow in God's Word together? There are all sorts of things both digital and in print, on a website and in an app. Things you can purchase or get for free. Curriculum, books, or one-off things. Classes you can offer, and more. This is a landscape that is ever-changing and increasing. What can you provide? What things can you share that they will be able to access on their own? What sort of contest could you challenge families with that has a fun prize at the end? I know you are creative enough to find the best solution to offer to your families. My challenge is to do it and make it readily available.

I've also seen many churches have suggested resources in an area of their kid's space. It looks like a bookshelf, sometimes. Other times it's a display with half a dozen resources they recommend to parents for their kids. If your church has a resource center, encourage them to feature one for kids each month. Will every family respond? Of course not. But what if a good portion of them choose to invest in the spiritual life of their child? Then, it's more than worth it.

Worship Nights for Generations

What can you do to provide a night for generations to worship together? As a parent, there's something pretty special when I can stand next to my son and worship with him. Watching him sing, close his eyes, and lift his hands melts my heart. How could you partner with other areas in your church to host a family worship night? Maybe parts of it could be led by different teams. Adults, students and children. It's important to have a mixture of songs that appeal to the different age spectrums. It's in that blend of styles and songs where the full experience of worshiping together happens. You also could bring in a special guest, like myself, who can lead this type of experience. This is where it's great to have those "home run" type songs that we discussed earlier. Include some hymns, as well. Invite everyone to get moving with a fun kid's song. Sing that popular worship song that can be heard on the radio as we speak. Have both kids and adults share the power of our worship. You may want to plan and align these worship nights seasonally or around holidays, like Christmas and Easter. Help families unite in living for the Lord by offering up their sacrifice of worship. It will be a beautiful time of gathering together to praise the Name above all names!

Brainstorm how you can partner with families beyond Sunday morning to lead kids, and empower those families in worship discipleship. Take one step at a time. You don't have to do all of these things next week, but what if you introduced each of them one at a time throughout the next six to twelve months? I think it would be really life-giving and beneficial. Form a routine of making these playlists, posts, and experiences available to parents on a regular basis. I have no doubt you'll be glad you empowered families to worship together. That one action will ultimately help them grow stronger as a unit and

Sweet Sound

will have lasting effects for years to come.

Be a Student
of Worship

I am fully convinced that you can't lead others to a place you haven't been. I'll also add to that: You can't lead others to a place you haven't been and aren't willing to go. If you want to lead worship well, then you must become a great worshiper. I'm not focused on when you're on stage for this one. I'm more concerned with how you worship when you're off stage. If you worship differently off stage then on stage, we have a problem.

David was a great worshiper because his worship was not conditional. He wasn't some diva who only worshiped when it was his turn to play the harp for the King. David poured out his worship when his heart was broken from the death of his child. I've seen famous worship leaders stand in the back like a punk with their hands in their pockets, as if they weren't moved. And, I've seen famous worship leaders laid out, face first, bowed down in adoring worship of the Lamb on the throne. Guess which one was more moving to see?

Make a choice and a habit to respond and worship well when you're the one being led. Whether you're in the back of the room or near the front, in a side section or up against the wall because there's not an open seat. If you're given an opportunity to worship, then engage in it. Be a great participator of worship. It's not enough to be a great facilitator of worship if you haven't learned how to be led by others first. Don't let the rocks cry out for you when you don't have a mic. Your worship is just as important off stage. It's likely telling a greater story than words could tell to your church family who sees your heart shining through your sacrifice of praise and gift of worship to your King.

Galatians 6:7 says, "A man reaps what he sows." It's a Biblical principle that you reap what you sow. I am convinced that if I want others to participate and engage when I'm the one *leading* worship, then it starts with me participating and fully engaging when I am the one being *led* in worship. If a worship leader invites people to stand, then stretch those legs and stand. Don't sit there after you were specifically told to stand. If a worship leader tells a congregation to lift their hands, lift your hands. What you sow, you reap. If I want to *reap* good participation, then I must first *sow* good participation. This is a Kingdom principle at work here.

Acts 3:20 tells us, "Times of refreshing come from the presence of the Lord." (ESV) Are you weary? Are you burdened? Are you worn out? Let's face it. There are times due to the busyness of ministry that we need a touch from Jesus. As adults, we walk through challenging seasons where we need to rest at the feet of Father God and remind ourselves that He is always good. In these moments, worship. Submerge your spirit in the presence of the One whose burden is light. Lay your burdens down and breathe in the understanding that He is God.

The global pandemic of 2020 taught me the lesson of "Be still, and know that I am God." (Psalm 46:10). I would've consistently told you that I trusted God to take care of me. But, as my calendar was wiped clean and two months turned into six, then nine months turned to a year, and beyond, so did a fraction of what I was used to doing.

I realized that my trust was more so in the calendar I had created for myself. As long as I could see things on the horizon, it was easy for me to "trust God." That entire time I had been trusting in my doing rather than His being. As time passed on and my live event schedule was practically dead, I learned to actually trust God in my stillness. As I spent more time without a microphone in my hand than I ever had in my life, I became more fully convinced of things I need to speak to this world.

In your role as worship leader, I believe it's crucial for you to become a student of worship. There's a variety of methods you can use to do that. The important thing is that you keep learning, seeking, and growing in your knowledge and understanding of worship. The more you know, the more you will have within you to share with others and lead them with. Here are a few things that have encouraged and challenged me through the years:

Books:
"Holy Roar" by Chris Tomlin & Darren Whitehead
"The Air I Breathe" by Louie Giglio
"Extravagant Worship" by Darlene Zschech
"The Reset" by Jeremy Riddle

Teachings:
Search "Aaron Keyes" on PursuitofGod.com
Steven Furtick's *"Bars & Battles"* series
Louie Giglio. He has so much to share on the subject.
Darrell Johnson's *"Something Changed in Heaven."* You can find it via "Worship Central" on YouTube. Put this message at the top of your list. Listen when you can be fully engaged because this lesson

is life-changing when you realize what's happening on the throne in Heaven.

Concerts/Worship Nights:

Go to special concerts and worship nights in your area. Whether they are put on by national touring acts or another local church in town. There are two layers here. First, it's an opportunity for you to be led in worship. As a leader, you can't only pour out. You also have to take in and fill yourself up, so you can be poured out again. My dad says it like this: "You have to make deposits in order to write checks." Second, what do you see that you could apply to what you do? How do they lead others well? Was there a cool transition or programming element that you could utilize in your own ministry? How do they invite the audience to enter in? I can go to a mainstream concert and learn something that I can apply to what I do on stage.

The same could apply for watching other churches online. Don't fall into a trap of comparison or trying to be something you're not. Those are the ditches on either side of the road. There's something pretty special in the middle, if you take the time to search it out. They are the universal characteristics of great leadership and musicianship that we can learn from and apply to our environment.

Follow worship leaders on **SOCIAL MEDIA**, as well. They will likely share tips on leading and insights on scriptures about worship that you can learn from.

Magazines and Webinars:

Subscribe to *Worship Musician Magazine* or *Worship Leader Magazine*. Tune into their webinars and learn one nugget at a time. Just as the principles that you teach shape the hearts and understanding of those you lead week after week, so do the opportunities you give your mind to learn from. They grow knowledge and spiritual depth.

Consider a **COACHING PROGRAM**. There are various worship and ministry coaching programs available. What do you need help with? What kind of challenge motivates you best? Do you need someone else in your life who will call out the depth of what is hidden in your heart? I have been given more opportunities to work with leaders, coaching them one-on-one in these areas. I'd love to connect and help you lead and disciple others.

May I remind you again to study **DAVID**? Read the Psalms. Soak up the example he was of a true worshiper in the hills and valleys. Study worship in **scripture**. You can find worship in the Christmas story and learn about the freedom that Paul & Silas' worship brought.

Ask God to speak to you and reveal things that you did not know. Tell Him you want to grow in your knowledge of worship and the power that it holds. Ask Him to speak. Open up your ears to listen. I promise your ask, plus your willingness to listen and obey, will draw the Father's heart to yours. May you overflow with knowledge, understanding, and revelation as you commit to leading others with what you've been given.

PRAY! Pray for direction as you lead worship. I believe God can speak to your heart and guide your decision-making as you plan and prepare your set during the week. He can also speak to you while you're on stage. He will likely do both. Just make sure you're carving out space for him to speak during the in between places.

Pray for the right people on your team. I believe he will send them. You will still need to recruit. You still need to inquire of your current team if they know of others who would be a great fit for what you do. You have a part to play in it, but I've also seen God respond to our request. What you do partnered with the power of your prayers is an incredible thing. Be specific in what you ask for. (You absolutely want them to have godly character. Talent and ability are needed, as well.)

Read the Word of God. The Bible is alive and it speaks to us. There are times when we come across the perfect verse at the perfect time and it feels as if it was a gift straight from God for where we are in that season. I remember asking Andy Chrisman, who was the worship pastor I served under, about what I heard spill out of him as he led. We'd get to a spontaneous worship moment at the end of a song or during a transition and I would hear Andy sing out these things that we hadn't rehearsed, yet sounded familiar. They were familiar because they were truths straight from scripture. One day I inquired about it, and he shared how he felt the responsibility to fill himself up with the Word so that the Word would spill out in those moments he was leading the congregation. Friends, that is good wisdom.

Did you know that discipling your family to worship is a qualification for leadership? 1 Timothy 3:4 says, "His heart should be set on guiding his household with wisdom and dignity, bringing up his children to worship with devotion and purity." (TPT) How you **lead your family** matters. There's nothing that makes my heart leap more than seeing my children connect with a song and participate in worship. I have some photos of beautiful moments where it just clicked. Their heart and body was postured for worship. I treasure those photos because I know they were getting it. Does this mean they look like spiritual ninjas daily? No, it's a process. There have been days where they got it wrong. There are times where correction was needed, as well as space for teaching moments to happen. We are still learning and talking. Modeling and teaching. One day and conversation at a time. I am committed to discipling my kids in worship, just as I am in helping to develop them into functioning members of society, as they find their God-given place in the world.

Build a **worship playlist for yourself.** Not just of the songs you need to do at church, but the songs you may never get to sing from stage that personally bless your heart. I'm talking about your favorite worship anthems. Are there songs from years ago that faded from the spotlight, but minister to your heart and lead you to the Father. There are songs I love that I led in past seasons that I may not get to lead much currently, but those songs help connect me to God's heart and the gift of worship I need to express. Build a playlist that you can listen to when you need to draw close to the Father. Use it as you enter in and make space for God to speak to you about what you're to do and the decisions you're making. The song could be "Great Is Thy Faithfulness" or "I Love You Lord." It may be "Shout to the Lord" or "Here I Am to Worship." It could be "Nothing Else" or "The Blessing." The years go by and the songs stack up. What's at the top of the charts changes every week of the year. On the streaming platforms, it fluctuates throughout the day. I don't care if it's by Keith Green or the current artist whose song is #1 on the CCLI chart. What I am saying is take some time to momentarily forget about your to-do list. Forget about what you need to learn and practice for Sunday. What are the songs that you feel were written just for you? Push play and express your worship with those. Draw near to God and He will draw near to you. One offering of worship at a time.

I'll end the same way I began. **You can't lead others to a place you've never been.** Go there first so you can effectively lead others there, too.

I am so thankful that you came on this journey with me. Thank you for caring enough about the spiritual development of those who you lead to read this book. You sensed there could be more so you read these pages. I thank God for you and will be praying for your leadership in the days to come.

Stay sensitive to His voice. I shared how, as a worship leader, there are times where I feel a nudge to go somewhere different or share something specific. I've had moments where I try to stick to the plan and ignore it, but oh so often I become aware that it is His voice. I know that if I choose not to follow, then I will be disobedient.

I am learning that in life all that matters is our obedience. I had a life-changing experience after going to see Ark Encounter, the place south of Cincinnati where they built a true to size replica of Noah's Ark. It was really, really BIG! The thing that I couldn't shake as my time there ended, and the thing I kept thinking about in the days thereafter, was that Noah obeyed. He believed God spoke to Him and told him to build the ark to keep him, his family, and all the animals safe, so he did it. There's no doubt that people thought he was crazy. Seeing the size in real life only confirmed this to me. He probably even thought he was a bit crazy in the process, at times. But even through their laughter, through their pointed fingers and judgment, as he most likely was the running joke of town, he kept on building. And we all know what happened once the project was done. When the last two animals entered the ark, the rain began to come down. Hear me testify that Noah *obeyed* God. You and I are here today because of Noah's obedience. We are able to lead kids in worship because Noah obeyed. What I began to see that day and in the months that followed is **the ripple effect of our obedience goes farther than we could ever**

imagine.

I don't believe it's by accident that you picked up this book. I pray that it changed you. Not just as a worship leader or ministry director, but as a follower of Jesus. I pray you know how rich and special your worship is and that you keep pouring it out as a costly fragrance for the King. I trust that God spoke to you and gave you a vision for what worship could be within and outside the walls of your church. I believe you've gained knowledge and a passion for discipling kids to be the worshipers who God made them to be. You have been equipped for such a time as this. To put these disciplines in action may very well be a step of obedience that you know you need to take. Because the choice to disobey that nudge, instead of embracing the revelation you've received with your YES, would surely be a failure you don't want your name attached to.

After my visit to the ark, I said "yes" to a music project I had been procrastinating because I didn't have the money to pay for it. But, after realizing I am here because Noah obeyed, I realized I didn't need any money to write the songs, finish up my ideas, and turn voice memos into completed songs. I actually had the finances to be able to record the songs, so I could at least start the process and book the studio time to record the audio. So, I started taking steps. Some were easy and some were really big steps of faith. For nearly a year, I moved forward in obedience, one task and checkmark at a time. I learned a mighty lesson about faith, obedience, and God's timing through it all. That process changed my life. I'm not the same Christian I was before that. I am a better one. My faith was stretched and strengthened.

We hear a lot about finishing our race well, and rightfully so. My heart breaks for so many, ministers included, who have not finished well what God put them on earth to do. Working through my own procrastination of what became the *Little Praise Party: Ready Set Go* project, I realized that so many never even *begin* the race they were called to run. You can't finish something you never begin. The way you start your race is crucial. As I wrote the song "Ready Set Go" and completed that project, I became pretty obsessed with checkered patterns. Think about a black and white checkered race flag, or it can be any color combination you come across. My challenge to you moving forward is that every time you see a checkered pattern to think about obedience. Remember that your obedience matters to God. What are the things that He is asking you to do, personally? He needs you to be obedient and run your race. In the long run, it matters more than you're able to currently see in the short term. Your life has a ripple effect greater than you could ever imagine.

The kids you lead in worship.

The families they represent.

Who they will become in the decades that follow.

How they will grow to impact this world for Jesus.

God is asking for your "yes" to run this race of discipling kids in worship.

It may be costly at times. It may move slower than you'd like at times. It may challenge you on occasion. But, I can promise that it will change and transform you as you move forward in obedience, step by step.

Hebrews 12:1-2 says, "Therefore, since we are surrounded by such a great cloud of witnesses, let us throw off everything that hinders and the sin that so easily entangles. And let us run with perseverance the race marked out for us, fixing our eyes on Jesus, the pioneer and perfecter of faith."

There are a few key points about these verses. We see that we are to get rid of the things that hinder us and hold us back. We are to get rid of the sin that can so easily entangle us. We are called to run our race focused, steady, and with perseverance. How do we do that? By fixing our eyes on Jesus. *He* alone is the author and perfecter of our faith.

I can think of no better way to help kids fix their eyes on Jesus than through worship. The songs that you sing. The words they declare. How you lead and invite them to enter into the presence of God Almighty. The playlists you share so their families can help them meditate on God's Word day and night. The environments you create so you can teach them to run toward God and surrender all that they are to declaring His greatness.

It is a race worthy of running. You are needed. You may never fully see this side of Heaven how important your YES is, but may I remind you that your YES is vital to the overall mission of the Church.

What you do isn't about surviving Sunday.

It's about their future.

Let's raise disciples who are fully engaged--mind, body, and spirit--in the worship they were created to give the Creator.

If you want to walk on water, then you have to first get out of the boat. Fix your eyes on Jesus.

Go disciple kids to fix their eyes on Jesus through times of worship. He created their worship to be powerful, and it is. Let it rise and go straight to the throne of Heaven.

Be after God's heart, just as David was.

Never forget that God ordained the powerful praise of children to be a sweet sound in His ear.

I believe in you and I'm cheering you on.

Ready...Set...GO!

References

Dykes, John Bacchus. "Holy, Holy, Holy." 1861.

Avalon. "I Don't Want to Go." 2001. Sparrow Records.

Tomlin, Chris. "I Stand Amazed." 2006. Passion Conferences.

Tomlin, Chris. "How Great is Our God." 2004. Sparrow Records.

Daniels, Charlie. "The Devil Went Down to Georgia." 1979. Epic.

Johnson, Darrell. *"Something Changed in Heaven."* 2019. youtube.com/watch?v=3hrFzI-qSdA

Johnny Rogers and Yancy. "Heartbeat: Teach the Heart of Worship." yancyministries.com/heartbeat

Miller, Stephen. *"Why Posture Matters in Worship."* Excerpt taken from The Gospel Coalition. thegospelcoalition.org/article/why-posture-matters-in-worship/

Tharp, Twyla. "The Creative Habit: Learn It and Use It for Life." 2009. Published by Simon & Schuster.

Yancy. "Trust & Believe" from Kidmin Worship Vol. 3.

Yancy. "Our God" from Kidmin Worship Vol. 2.

Amber Sky Records. "Happy and You Know It." 2011 OrangeKidsMusic.com.

Yancy. "There is Power" from Kidmin Worship Vol. 4.

Yancy. "We Believe" from Kidmin Worship Vol. 4.

Yancy. "Strength & Shield" from Kidmin Worship Vol. 6.

Yancy. "Glory To Your Name" from Kidmin Worship Vol. 6.

Yancy. "Who You Say I Am." Yancy Ministries Single.

Yancy. "Good Good Father" from Kidmin Worship Vol. 4..

Yancy. "Not Ashamed" from Jesus Music Box.

Yancy. "What a Beautiful Name" from Kidmin Worship Vol. 6.

Yancy. "Oceans" from Kidmin Worship Vol. 2.

Yancy. "Praise the Lord Every Day" from Little Praise Party: Taste and See.

Yancy. "Hosanna Rock." 2012. Yancy Ministries.

Yancy. "I Like To" from Little Praise Party: Happy Day Everyday.

Yancy. "Brand New Day" from Little Praise Party: Happy Day Everyday.

Yancy. "If You're Happy and You Know It." Little Praise Party: My Best Friend.

Yancy. "My Best Friend." Little Praise Party: My Best Friend.

Yancy. "Forever and Ever" from Stars, Guitars & Megaphone Dreams.

Yancy. "Better Than The Best Thing" from Jesus Music Box.

Yancy. "Alive" from Kidmin Worship Vol. 2.

"Joy to the World" is a popular Christmas carol with words by Isacc Watts. The words of the hymn are based on Psalm 98, Psalm 96, and Genesis 3." Source: Wikipedia.

Dion, Celine. "My Heart Will Go On." 1997. Columbia Records. Epic.

Wideman, Jim. *Out of the Mouth of Babes.* Article in KidzMatter magazine. July/August 2014 issue.

Yancy. "Father Abraham" from Little Praise Party: My Best Friend.

Yancy. "Sunday School Rock" from Little Praise Party: My Best Friend.

Yancy. "Shout" from Little Praise Party: Happy Day Every.

Yancy. "God is So Good" from Little Praise Party: My Best Friend.

Yancy. "Ready Set Go" from Little Praise Party: Ready Set Go.

Yancy. "The Bath Song" from Little Praise Party: My Best Friend.

Yancy. "Super Wonderful" from Little Praise Party: Taste and See.

Yancy. "My God is Number One" from Little Praise Party: Taste and See.

"Waffle and Wiggles: Preschool Concerts." Yancy Ministries. https://yancyministries.com/waffles-wiggles-preschool-concerts-creating-family-memories/

Tomlin, Chris. Whitehead, Darren. "Holy Roar: 7 Words That Will Change The Way You Worship." 2017. Bowyer & Bow.

Giglio, Louie. "The Air I Breathe: Worship as a Way of Life." 2003. Multnomah Books.

Zschech, Darlene. "Extravagant Worship." 2004. Bethany House Publishers.

Riddle, Jeremy. "The Reset: Returning to the Heart of Worship and a Life of Undivided Devotion." 2020. Jeremy Riddle.

Keyes, Aaron. http://www.pursuitofgod.com/sermonsearch.aspx?sermonsite_action=view_authors&sermonsite_rowkey=Aaron+Keyes

Furtrick, Steven. *"Bars and Battles"* sermon series. Elevation Church. https://www.youtube.com/playlist?list=PLetEMD1Ss0PA1Tbz2PpaQlQSWpqEkSd9O

Chisholm, Thomas. "Great is Thy Faithfulness." 1923.

Yancy. "I Love You, Lord" from Little Praise Party: Taste and See.

Zschech, Darlene. "Shout to the Lord." 2010. Hillsong Worship.

Hughes, Tim. "Here I Am To Worship." 2001. EMI Gospel Records.

Yancy. "Nothing Else" from Nothing Else single.

Kari Jobe, Cody Carnes, and Elevation Worship. "The Blessing." 2020. Provident Label Group.

Yancy. "Little Praise Party: Ready Set Go." 2020. Yancy Ministries.

All song arrangements by Yancy available at YancyMinistries.com

Acknowledgements

To the ones who came before me, blazing the trail and personally impacting my life along the way:

Ernie & Debbie Rettino (Psalty)

Peter and Hanneke Jacobs (Colby)

Rob C. Evans (The Donut Man)

Ken Blount (Nicodemus)

Ronnie Caldwell

Alan Root Robertson

David & Beci Wakerley (Hillsong Kids)

Charlie Bancroft (Uncle Charlie)

Thank you for the cups of cold water you gave to children in the form of lyrics and melodies. I see now how you humbled yourself and even your talent level because you saw a need. Thank you for the Word of God you put in your songs to build the faith of those who listened, and how you put His praises on their lips. Your reward in Heaven will be great. I honor each one of you.

Michayla White, I believed I could because you first told me I should. I'll never forget our dinner over tacos. The things you said that night still echo in my mind. I don't know all that the future holds but I'm so thankful that Jesus placed you in my life to encourage me to offer up my "yes," with confetti, of course.

Stephanie Hughes, I know this relationship is God-ordained. I met my match in a girl who can make a social media post about fashion also be spiritual. Thank you so much for editing this book with such care. You guarded the message that Holy Spirit had breathed into me and entrusted me to share. In the process, you encouraged my confidence by championing my writing ability to relinquish my fears and instead trust that I was made for this. I'm forever thankful.

Amanda Ferrin, you inspire me. Thank you for believing "Worshiping kids will change the world." I pray your fire and understanding of the power of kids worship will be replicated in the life of every leader who reads this book.

Kari Jobe, you sang over nearly every word of this book as I listened to your "The Blessing Live" album. No matter what place I was in, through my air pods you created a tangible atmosphere of worship and underscored the message I was writing by ushering in His presence. Thank you for the authority that you lead others with. I can't wait for the day we are all in His 'throne room' worshiping together.

Mark Campbell, thank you for being a sounding board offering up wisdom and, on some occasions, a place to vent. I'm grateful God placed you on my team and am always humbled by your belief in what I do and create. I appreciate all your hard work in proclaiming the message about the projects God has me create.

My family is the greatest support system and team to do life and ministry with:

Mom & Dad, you've always believed in me. The sacrifices you have made on my behalf are far too many to count. I believe that I have the best parents in the world and I'm not just saying that. I know that I would not have become even an ounce of what I have without your prayers, guidance and example. Thank you for the costly outpouring of ministry you have demonstrated. Your commitment to live according to the Word, no matter what, is a legacy that I am honored to be a part of and carry into future generations of our family. I always want to make you proud.

Whitney, thank you for being by my side as a sister and an assistant. I appreciate all your help with the boys while I ran away to coffee shops to write this book. Thank you for serving Yancy Ministries and helping me make Jesus loud.

Cory, you release me to fly and I'm forever grateful you're by my side. Whatever the season, you allow me to run the race God has called me to. That means so much and I love you forever.

Sparrow and Rhythm, I am so proud to be your mom. I love watching you fall in love with Jesus. I pray that you'll be boys just like David who always know where their help comes from. May you live your life with the same confidence in our God and a reflex to worship Him no matter what. Allow who you are and the things you do to be after God's heart each and every day. In doing so, you'll grow to be the men I dream you will one day be.

Jesus, You are my why. I love You so much and I truly want this world to know how good You are. Thank You for the revelation You have imparted to me about worship. It's an action we take and it's an offering we give. You are the One who created children to have powerful worship. May we never forget it is part of Your plan. You've entrusted this message to me to be a conduit to help others have renewed minds of understanding. I am expectant for the mending of broken hearts and bodies made whole in Your presence. I believe as the spark of worship is ignited in our churches, revival will be experienced. I speak to dry bones and tell them to come alive. Thank You for the gift of music and this expression of love that we get to give You here on earth, but also for eternity in Heaven. This is all for You!

Yancy is a worship leader, songwriter and producer of hundreds of songs that *make Jesus loud*. She has traveled the globe performing family concerts and leading worship. Her Dove Award winning music is *all the things kids love and everything adults value. As a songwriter, she's written a number one song, "I Don't Want to Go," recorded by Avalon. She loves the local church and is a powerhouse at leading and teaching kids to worship.*

Continually a popular worship resource in churches and homes around the world, the "Little Praise Party" series is focused on inviting young hearts to a relationship with Jesus by beginning a foundation of theology through the discipline of worship. Yancy writes these songs and crafts these arrangements with an intentional focus on this phase of life. "Little Praise Party" features animated music videos designed specifically for preschoolers and younger elementary children. Families love to watch these on Minno, RightNow Media, Yippee, Smile of the Child, YouTube, and more. Favorite songs include: "Hosanna Rock," "Praise the Lord Every Day" and "Stop & Go." The series "Kidmin Worship" is the ultimate church worship resource of lyric videos, motion tutorials, and more for preteen and elementary kids. It includes age-specific arrangements of hymns and popular worship songs, as well as original songs such as "Super Wonderful," "Strength & Shield," and "Live Differently." Developed from a passion to teach kids the heart of worship, she created "Heartbeat," a five-lesson curriculum that highlights David's example and heart of worship. These lessons have been a game-changer for churches across the country.

Yancy is a passionate advocate of raising disciples to worship.

She has authority in this area because of her faithful commitment to the promise in scripture that the worship of children is power-filled. She authored "Sweet Sound: The Power of Discipling Kids in Worship" to help you create a rhythm of worship in your church. Its message is the cry of her heart and ministry.

With a family legacy of children's ministry, she's the daughter of children's ministry pioneer, Jim Wideman. Her unique PK perspective helps encourage and champion the Kidmin community that the seeds they are planting will reap a harvest that will go on to affect families for generations. Yancy lives in Nashville, TN with her husband, Cory, and sons, Sparrow and Rhythm.

Listen to all of Yancy's music at your favorite music source.
Follow Yancy on Social Media: @YancyNotNancy

Bring Yancy to your church. Yancy loves helping create memories for families. YancyMinistries.com/events

Get Yancy's game-changing resources for your church.
KidminWorship.com
YancyMinistries.com/ReadySetGo
YancyMinistries.com/Heartbeat

Learn about coaching and other books by Yancy at
YancyMinistries.com